MW01290154

Bible Study Guide

Matthew 1 - 13

Good Questions Have
Small Groups Talking

By Josh Hunt

Contents

Lesson #1, Matthew 3.1 - 10
Good Questions Have Groups Talking
www.joshhunt.com

Matthew 3.1 - 10

OPEN

Let me ask each of you to share your name, and, have you ever spent the night in the wilderness?

DIG

1. **Where did John minister? See if you can find it on a map. Better yet, if you have a smart phone or tablet, do a search for a picture.**

John's ministry was carried out in the desert (cf. 3:3; 4:1; 11:7; 15:33) of Judea, the barren area just west of the Dead Sea. This largely uninhabited area is characterized by a dry climate and a topography featuring valleys (wadis) running from the hills in the west to the geological Rift Valley of the Jordan River and Dead Sea in the east. During the rainy season, these wadis become swift streams, but they are largely dry the rest of the year (cf. 7:26–27). Therefore, the NLT's translation "wilderness" should not be understood as a forest or jungle. The role of the wilderness in redemptive history as the place of refuge, testing, the Exodus, and the giving of the law may be significant here. — David Turner and Darrell L. Bock, *Cornerstone Biblical Commentary, Vol 11: Matthew and Mark* (Carol Stream, IL: Tyndale House Publishers, 2005), 57.

2. **Context. We tend to think that in Bible days there were prophets constantly speaking to the people. Think of the context. When was the most recent time there was a prophet in Israel?**

The emergence of John was like the sudden sounding of the voice of God. At this time the Jews were sadly conscious that the voice of the prophets spoke no more. They said that for four hundred years there had been no prophet. Throughout long centuries the voice of prophecy had been silent. As they put it themselves, "There was no voice, nor any that answered." But in John the prophetic voice spoke again. What then were the characteristics of John and his message? — *Barclay's Daily Study Bible (NT).*

3. **Overview. What do you know about John? How would you characterize his ministry?**

He fearlessly denounced evil wherever he might find it. If Herod the king sinned by contracting an evil and unlawful marriage, John rebuked him. If the Sadducees and Pharisees, the leaders of orthodox religion, the churchmen of their day, were sunk in ritualistic formalism, John never hesitated to say so. If the ordinary people were living lives which were unaware of God, John would tell them so. Wherever John saw evil—in the state, in the Church, in the crowd—he fearlessly rebuked it. He was like a light which lit up the dark places; he was like wind which swept from God throughout the country. It was said of a famous journalist who was great, but who never quite fulfilled the work he might have done, "He was perhaps not easily enough disturbed." There is still a place in the Christian message for warning and denunciation. "The truth," said Diogenes, "is like the light to sore eyes." "He who never offended anyone," he said, "never did anyone any good." It may be that there have been times when the Church was too careful not to offend. There come occasions when the time for smooth politeness has gone, and the time for blunt rebuke has come.

(ii) He urgently summoned men to righteousness. John's message was not a mere negative denunciation; it was a positive erecting of the moral standards of God. He not only denounced men for what they had done; he summoned them to what they ought to do. He not only condemned men for what they were; he challenged them to be what they could be. He was like a voice calling men to higher things. He not only rebuked evil, he also set before men the good. It may well be that there have been times when the Church was too occupied in telling men what not to do; and too little occupied in setting before them the height of the Christian ideal.

(iii) John came from God. He came out of the desert. He came to men only after he had undergone years of lonely preparation by God. As Alexander Maclaren said, "John leapt, as it were, into the arena full-grown and full-armed." He came, not with some opinion of his own, but with a message from God. Before he spoke to men, he had companied long with God. The preacher, the teacher with the prophetic voice, must always come into the presence of men out of the presence of God.

(iv) John pointed beyond himself. The man was not only a light to illumine evil, a voice to rebuke sin, he was also a signpost to God. It was not himself he wished men to see; he wished to prepare them for the one who was to come. It was the Jewish belief that Elijah would return before the Messiah came, and that he would t)e the herald of the coming King. "Behold I will send you Elijah the prophet before the great and terrible day of the Lord comes" (Mal 4:5). John wore a garment of camel's hair, and a leathern belt around his waist. That is the very description of the raiment which Elijah had worn (2 Ki 1:8). Matthew connects him with a prophecy from Isaiah (Isa 40:3). In ancient times in the East the roads were bad. There was an eastern proverb which said, "There are three states of misery—sickness, fasting and travel." Before a traveller set out upon a journey he was advised "to pay all debts, provide for dependents, give parting gifts, return all articles under trust, take money and good-temper for the journey; then bid farewell to all." The ordinary roads were no better than tracks. They were not surfaced at all because the soil of Palestine is hard and will bear the traffic of mules and asses and oxen and carts. A journey along such a road was an adventure, and indeed an undertaking to be avoided. There were some few surfaced and artificially made roads. Josephus, for instance, tells us that Solomon laid a causeway of black basalt stone along the roads that lead to Jerusalem to make them easier for the pilgrims, and "to manifest the grandeur of his riches and government." All such surfaced and artificially-made roads were originally built by the king and for the use of the king. They were called "the king's highway." They were kept in repair only as the king needed them for any journey that he might make. Before the king was due to arrive in any area, a message was sent out to the people to get the king's roads in order for the king's journey. John was preparing the way for the king. The preacher, the teacher with the prophetic voice, points not at himself, but at God. His aim is not to focus men's eyes on his own cleverness, but on the majesty of God. The true preacher is obliterated in his message.

Men recognized John as a prophet, even after years when no prophetic voice had spoken, because he was a light to light up evil things, a voice to summon men to righteousness, a signpost to point men to God, and because he had in him that unanswerable authority which clings to the man who comes into the presence of men out of the presence of God. — *Barclay's Daily Study Bible (NT).*

4. Verse 2. Repent is a word we use in church a lot. What exactly does it mean?

The Bible says, "God has commanded men everywhere to repent." Jesus said, "Unless you repent, you too will all perish" (Luke 13:5, NIV).

So obviously "repent" is a pivotal word. But what does it mean?

It means to "change" or to "turn." It's like driving down the highway, pulling a U-turn, and heading the other direction. More than simply being sorry, it is a word of action. Many people feel remorse for their sin but never truly repent.

Remorse is being sorry, repentance is being sorry enough to stop.

Paul wrote: "God can use sorrow in our lives to help us turn away from sin and seek salvation. We will never regret that kind of sorrow. But sorrow without repentance is the kind that results in death" (2 Corinthians 7:10, NLT).

In the story of the prodigal son, the young man knew he was wrong—probably knew it from the beginning. But nothing changed until he acted on that knowledge, crawled out of the pig pen, and started down the road toward his father and home. He had a "change of mind" that resulted in a "change of direction." — Greg Laurie, *10 Things You Should Know about God and Life* (Dana Point, CA: Kerygma Publishing—Allen David Books, 2011).

5. Is repentance something we do once or many times?

This is the message the world needs, but it is also the message the church needs. This is why we find this theme of repentance in all the letters of the New Testament. Christians who have repented must continue to live lives of repentance (e.g., 2 Corinthians 7:9, 10; 12:21; 2 Peter 3:9). Do you remember the seven letters to the seven churches in Revelation 2, 3? Each church gets a unique message dealing with its specific issue, yet one message that is given to five of the seven is "repent" (2:5, 16, 21, 22; 3:3, 17). So, what John the Baptist says in verse 8, "Bear fruit in keeping with repentance," and in verse 11, "I baptize you with water for repentance," and verse 2, "Repent, for the kingdom of heaven is at hand" is a relevant message for the world and for the church today. — Douglas Sean O'Donnell, *Matthew: All Authority in Heaven and on Earth, ed. R. Kent Hughes, Preaching the Word* (Wheaton, IL: Crossway, 2013), 70.

6. What good things come to those who repent?

WHEN MY WIFE AND I lived in Hyde Park in Chicago, near the University of Chicago, a chemistry professor was part of our congregation. Every Sunday night he and his wife would invite college students and other young adults over for a nice informal dinner. When you walked through their front door there was a small, decorative sign that had one simple word written in large block letters: REPENT.

I have often thought about that sign, and I have been tempted from time to time to duplicate it, or maybe even expand upon it, in our home—perhaps to have in the entranceway, "REPENT," and then in the living room "FROM THE WRATH TO COME," and finally in the dining room, "I REALLY MEAN IT!" But I have not yet gained the courage to do so, for such a message is so at odds with our culture. I can't think of a word—other than perhaps wrath or Hell—that has such a negative connotation. And I can't think of a word, of all the ones we find often in our Bibles, that is so seldom found on our lips. Maybe this quiet and quirky chemistry professor, with his Ivy League education and his years of scientific study, was like most accomplished scientists, a bit mad. Or maybe we're the ones who are off our rockers because we are afraid of what the world might think of us. We are afraid that if we were to have on our doorposts, walls, or lips the message of John the Baptist the world might call us crazy.

However, this message of repentance—turning from self and sin to God and grace—is what the world needs. And this is why each time the gospel is preached by the apostles (and here I'm thinking specifically of the sermons we find in Acts), the one application made in every message is "repent" (e.g., Acts 2:38; 3:19; 5:31; 8:22; 17:30; 26:20; cf. 11:18; 20:21). From Peter's message to the Jews in Jerusalem to Paul's before the Greeks in Athens, the message is the same: God "commands all people everywhere to repent" (Acts 17:30). — Douglas Sean O'Donnell, *Matthew: All Authority in Heaven and on Earth*, ed. R. Kent Hughes, *Preaching the Word* (Wheaton, IL: Crossway, 2013), 69–70.

7. John taught that the kingdom God has come near. It is here—now. What exactly is the kingdom of God?

The "kingdom of God" is really just a natural extension of shalom. The phrase comes from the Greek word basileia, which translates as "rule" or "authority."

When Jesus is King, we experience shalom. Whatever the King touches becomes redeemed and moves toward fullness of life. The markers of shalom become abundance, beauty, respect, dignity, equality, health, vitality, and holistic flourishing.

But when Jesus is not our king, we experience a loss of shalom. This can manifest as anything from internal struggle (depression, anxiety, insecurity, self-centeredness) to physical struggle (sickness, disease), neighborhood struggle (violence, crime, poor educational options, lack of access to healthy food), national struggle (racism, oppression, lack of access to jobs or capital), and global struggle (war, famine, abject poverty).

Our intuition tells us that God created the world to work a certain way, and our spirits hope and pray that Jesus is working to restore creation to its original potential. We "groan inwardly," along with the rest of creation, as we await this restoration (see Rom. 8:22–23).

The Garden of Eden was our first glimpse of shalom. We got to see what the world looked like when God was in control. We got to see how God related to humans and how the entire created ecosystem reflected God's glory. We all possess a distant memory of that shalom, and everything inside of us longs to return to that.

Though sin and selfishness wreaked havoc on that shalom, that was not the end of the story. God initiated a healing and restoration project, and the death and resurrection of Jesus Christ was the pinnacle of that plan. Jesus is "the image of the invisible God," as Paul says in Colossians 1:15, and through him the invisible God becomes visible for all of us to see.

Image bearers

Through the resurrected Jesus the kingdom of God is now being ushered in, and that is a full-scale restoration project. There is no aspect of our world that is untouched by Jesus, as Paul says in the next verse: "For in him all things were created: things in heaven and on earth, visible and invisible, whether thrones or powers or rulers or authorities; all things have been created through him and for him" (Col. 1:16).

The manifestation of the kingdom of God is initiated by Jesus, and his goal is fullness of life: "For God was pleased to have all his fullness dwell in him, and through him to reconcile to himself all things, whether things on earth or things in heaven, by making peace through his blood, shed on the cross" (Col. 1:19–20).

When Jesus shed his blood on the cross, he began the process of "making peace," the same word that he used when sending the disciples out on mission. This is what begins to bring the whole picture together. When we pray about, talk about, and work toward the kingdom of God, we are joining with this process of Jesus making peace through his blood, shed on the cross. — Daniel Hill, John Ortberg, and Nancy Ortberg, *10:10: Life to the Fullest* (Grand Rapids, MI: Baker, 2014).

8. **Do a search for the phrase, "Kingdom of God," or "Kingdom of Heaven." How common (read: important) is this teaching in the Bible?**

Jesus came to establish a kingdom, to ignite a revolution.

We learn a lot about that revolution by studying the life of its founder. What was Jesus known for?

Love.

He loved people no one else would love. His love was so radical, it restored souls and turned lives upside down. Time and time again, Jesus made the march of love.

We learn more about the revolution by examining its motto. Jesus lived before the time of Madison Avenue and Christian bookstores, so his slogan was not screamed by salesmen on TV commercials, nor was it printed on cheesy T-shirts, pens, or mints. Even still, his revolution had a creed: Love God, love people.

But that's not enough detail for my Ginsu knife–sharp intellect. I have a National Enquirer, inquiring-minds-need-to-know desire for more about this revolution. So what is the kingdom of God really like?

Fortunately, Jesus once posed that exact question. He said, "What is the kingdom of God like? What shall I compare it to? It is like a mustard seed, which a man took and planted in his garden. It grew and became a tree, and the birds of the air perched in its branches."

Jesus loved to tell ordinary-sounding stories that had a spiritual point. And almost always these stories had at least one element of surprise.

Remember, Jesus took center stage with the words, "The time has come. The kingdom of God is near." One hundred eleven times the Bible records Jesus saying the word kingdom. — Vince Antonucci, *Guerrilla Lovers: Changing the World with Revolutionary Compassion* (Grand Rapids, MI: Baker, 2010).

9. Is it possible to be saved and want nothing to do with life in the kingdom?

The idea that you can trust Christ for the hereafter but have no intention to obey him now is an illusion generated by a widespread unbelieving "Christian culture." In fact, you can no more trust Jesus and not intend to obey him than you can trust your doctor and not intend to follow his or her advice. If you don't intend to follow the advice, you simply don't trust the person. — Dallas Willard and Don Simpson, *Revolution of Character: Discovering Christ's Pattern for Spiritual Transformation* (Colorado Springs, CO: NavPress, 2005), 76.

10. Romans 14.17. What is the kingdom of God like?

The thief this verse [John 10.10] is referring to is the enemy of sheep—bears, lions, and wolves. Their goal is to kill and eat the sheep. But in contrast to that wicked agenda is the plan of our Shepherd, Jesus. He wants us to "have life, and have it to the full." In the next verse, Jesus offers a description of himself as the Good Shepherd: "I am the good shepherd. The good shepherd lays down his life for the sheep" (verse 11). The word "good" Jesus used here is full of meaning. Not only does it mean good as in morally good, but it also means "beautiful, winsome, lovely, attractive." So Jesus is the beautiful, winsome, lovely, attractive Shepherd. And this Good Shepherd's primary objective is to tend his flock as they flourish, are well-fed and cared for, are content and satisfied. He tells us as his followers, "Do not be afraid, little flock, for your Father has been pleased to give you the kingdom" (Luke 12:32). And the kingdom of God, we are told in Romans 14:17, is one "of righteousness, peace and joy in the Holy Spirit." — Greg Laurie, *Walking with Jesus: Daily Inspiration from the Gospel of John* (Grand Rapids, MI: Baker, 2007).

11. Matthew 13.31. How is the kingdom of God like a mustard seed?

One hundred eleven times the Bible records Jesus saying the word kingdom. And now he asks, "What is the kingdom of God like? What shall I compare it to?"

A mustard seed.

Surprise!

When a mustard seed grows it becomes a weed. It's a vine-like weed which will grow and grow and will intertwine with other weeds. And they'll continue to grow. And then they'll come into contact with a flower, which will be overtaken by the weeds. Now they're growing more. Soon they'll touch a tomato plant, and pretty soon that tomato plant has been overtaken by the weeds.

In fact, Jewish law at the time of Jesus made it illegal to plant mustard seed in a garden. Why was it against the law? Because they knew that it would grow and grow, invade the vegetables and other plants, and eventually take over the garden. If you let mustard in, eventually you'd be left with only mustard. The secret to gardening for the Jewish people of Jesus's day was: keep the mustard out!

I wonder how people reacted when they heard Jesus compare his kingdom to mustard seed planted in a garden. Did they just look shocked? Are you serious? Don't you know about mustard? Or did they giggle? This guy is hysterical. I can't wait to hear what he's going to say next! Or perhaps they frowned and thought, Jesus, hush. We like you, and if you keep comparing your kingdom to mustard, you're going to get yourself killed.

Jesus used a notorious, forbidden weed to describe God's kingdom. He said God's kingdom is like a man who planted a mustard seed in his garden. But people didn't plant mustard seed in gardens. It was illegal. If you did, the mustard seed would grow and grow and take over the entire garden.

I've tried to think of modern-day equivalents. If Jesus was here today and asked, "What is the kingdom of God like? What shall I compare it to?" what would he say next? What modern-day metaphor would make the same point and have similar shock value?

Maybe: "What is the kingdom of God like? What shall I compare it to? It is like a vicious computer virus a man sent out in an email from his computer, and it spread and spread and infected more and more and more computers."

Or perhaps this: "What is the kingdom of God like? What shall I compare it to? It is like AIDS, which infected one person but soon spread and spread and became an epidemic as scores of people received it."

If we heard that, our heads would spin. We'd say, "What? Are you serious?" And the people who heard Jesus back then would have reacted the same way. — Vince Antonucci,

Guerrilla Lovers: Changing the World with Revolutionary Compassion (Grand Rapids, MI: Baker, 2010).

12. Verse 4. Why do you suppose God led John to dress and eat as he did?

Locusts are the only type of insect permitted as food in the Mosaic law (Lev 11:20–23; cf. CD 12:14–15; 11QTemple 48:3–5 for their use as food at Qumran, roasted or boiled); they are still eaten by those in whose lands they flourish. Bonnard, 34, speaks with remarkable authority on the subject: "This insect was highly prized as nourishment, either in water and salt like our prawns, or dried in the sun and preserved in honey and vinegar, or powdered and mixed with wheat flour into a pancake." For honey found in the wild cf. Judg 14:8–9; 1 Sam 14:25–26 and the OT description of Palestine as "a land flowing with milk and honey." John's diet represents the attempt to live, like Bannus (see n. 35 above), on "food which grew by itself."40 His diet is compatible with that of a Nazirite.

In so far as John's clothing was meant to evoke a prophetic image, it corresponds to the way he was popularly perceived, as a prophet (11:9; 16:14; 21:26). It is sometimes stated that first-century Jews believed that prophecy had ceased with Malachi, whose book concludes with the promise of the eschatological return of Elijah, so that to identify John (and later Jesus) as a prophet was to make a quite stupendous claim. But it is more probable that the idea of the cessation of prophecy was confined to only one strand of rabbinic thinking, and that in popular thought the title "prophet" would not have been so unthinkable; Josephus' accounts of popular leaders who claimed to be prophets at this period indicate as much. — R. T. France, *The Gospel of Matthew, The New International Commentary on the New Testament* (Grand Rapids, MI: Wm. B. Eerdmans Publication Co., 2007), 106–107.

13. Verse 7 introduces the Pharisees and Sadducees. What do you know about these two groups?

The exact manner in which, and the exact date when, these parties rose is obscure. There is reason to believe, however, that the Pharisees were the successors of the ḥaṣidhim, i.e., the Pious or Saints. The latter were those Jews who, during and even prior to the Maccabean revolt (see pp. 127, 157), had opposed the adoption of Greek culture and customs. It is understandable that as long as the Maccabeans in their heroic struggle were chiefly motivated by religious principles they would have the full support of the ḥaṣidhim; but that when, especially during the days of John Hyrcanus and those who followed him, the emphasis of the Jewish rulers was shifted from the spiritual to the secular sphere, the ḥaṣidhim would either lose interest and withdraw themselves or else would actively oppose the descendants of the very people whom they had formerly supported. The Pharisees, meaning Separatists, may well have been, in their origin, the reformed or reorganized ḥaṣidhim, the ḥaṣidhim under another name. They separated themselves not only from the heathen, from publicans and from sinners, but even in general, from the indifferent Jewish mutltitudes, whom they derisively dubbed "the people who do not know the law" (John 7:49). They tried hard not to become contaminated or defiled by associating with anyone or anything that would render them ceremonially unclean.

The Sadducees were in many ways the very opposites of the Pharisees. They were the compromisers, the men who, though ostensibly still clinging to the law of God, were not really hostile to the spread of Hellenism. They were the sacerdotal party, the party to which the highpriests generally belonged. It is not surprising that it became popular to derive the name Sadducees from Zadok (LXX: Sadok), an etymology that may be correct. This Zadok was the man who during David's reign shared the highpriestly office with Abiathar (2 Sam. 8:17; 15:24; 1 Kings 1:35), and was made sole highpriest by Solomon (1 Kings 2:35). Until the days of the Maccabees the descendants of Zadok had retained the highpriesthood.
— William Hendriksen and Simon J. Kistemaker, *Exposition*

of the Gospel According to Matthew, vol. 9, New Testament Commentary (Grand Rapids: Baker Book House, 1953–2001), 201–202.

14. How did these two groups differ?

One important point on which the two parties clashed is clearly brought out in Acts 23:6–8:

"Paul, realizing that one section of the Sanhedrin were Sadducees and the other Pharisees, raised his voice and said to them, 'Brothers, I am a Pharisee and the son of Pharisees. It is with respect to the hope of the resurrection of the dead that I am being examined.' And when he had said this there arose a dissension between the Pharisees and the Sadducees, and the assembly was divided. For the Sadducees say that there is no resurrection or angel or spirit, but the Pharisees accept them all." From Josephus we learn that the Sadducees denied the immortality of the soul along with the resurrection of the body. They held that the soul perished when the body died.

Another point on which the two went in opposite directions had to do with the canon. The Pharisees recognized two criteria or standards for doctrine and discipline: the written Old Testament and the oral traditions. As to the latter, they believed that these additions to—but in reality often rather peculiar interpretations of—the written law had been given by Moses to the elders and had by the latter been transmitted orally down through the generations. They made so much of these traditions that often, by means of their emphasis upon them, they "made the word of God of no effect" (Matt. 15:6; Mark 7:13). The Sadducees, on the contrary, accepted nothing but Scripture. They esteemed the Pentateuch above the prophets, etc.

Finally, if Josephus, who at the age of nineteen had publicly joined the Pharisees, can be trusted, there was still another sharp contrast: the Pharisees believed not only in man's freedom and responsibility with respect to his own actions but also in the divine decree; the Sadducees rejected the decree (Josephus, Jewish War II.162–166; Antiquities

XIII.171–173, 297, 298; XVIII.12–17). — William Hendriksen and Simon J. Kistemaker, *Exposition of the Gospel According to Matthew, vol. 9, New Testament Commentary* (Grand Rapids: Baker Book House, 1953–2001), 202–203.

15. What did they have in common?

Though they differed so strikingly, yet basically many of these Pharisees and Sadducees were in perfect agreement, for in the final analysis they both tried to attain security by their own efforts: whether this security consisted in earthly possessions on this side of the grave, as with the Sadducees, many of whom were rich landowners and/or beneficiaries of the trade carried on in the temple precincts; or, on the other side (at least also on the other side), as with the Pharisees, who were striving with all their might to work their way into heaven. Religion in both cases was outward conformity, through self-effort, to a certain standard.

It should not be a matter of surprise, therefore, that when Jesus, with his emphasis on the religion of the heart and on God as the sole Author of salvation, appeared upon the scene of history he was rejected by both groups: by the Pharisees because he denounced them since they cleansed only the outside of the cup or platter (Matt. 23:25), and, while tithing mint, anise, and cummin, neglected the weightier matters of the law: "justice, and mercy, and fidelity" (23:23); and by the Sadducees because, by means of the temple-cleansing, he exposed their money-grabbing racket, and probably also because they considered his claims to pose a threat to the status quo of the nation and therefore to their own influential position. Besides, it is understandable that both Pharisees and Sadducees envied Jesus (Matt. 27:18).

So at last Pharisees and Sadducees co-operate to bring about his death (16:1, 6, 11; 22:15, 23; 26:3, 4, 59; 27:20). Even afterward they combine in their attempt to prevent belief in his resurrection (27:62). It is not strange, therefore, that Jesus would at times in one breath condemn both groups (16:6 ff). — William Hendriksen and Simon J. Kistemaker, *Exposition of the Gospel According to Matthew, vol. 9, New Testament*

Commentary (Grand Rapids: Baker Book House, 1953–2001), 203.

16. Verse 8. In addition to repentance, what else must the Pharisees and Sadducees do to enter the kingdom of God?

Furthermore, repentance must be validated as being real through fruit in one's life. Talk is cheap. Hypocrisy is real. John will not tolerate any religious game-playing simply to gain a following. He articulates a theme that will characterize Jesus' ministry as well. The evidence of real inner spiritual life is always the fruit of a changed external life. The arrival of the kingdom will bring with it real spiritual life that produces change from the inside out. Jesus says later that false disciples are those who do not have the life of the true vine. They are dead branches, good only to be thrown into the fire (John 15:6). The decisive identifying mark of a living tree is the fruit that it bears. The decisive identifying mark of the kingdom of God is a life that has repented from sin and bears the fruit of repentance (cf. Paul's message in Acts 26:20). — Michael J. Wilkins, *Matthew, The NIV Application Commentary* (Grand Rapids, MI: Zondervan Publishing House, 2004), 136–137.

17. Why is it necessary for fruit to accompany repentance?

The CEO of a major airline had nearly completed negotiations with his pilots, flight attendants, and mechanics, who had conceded to take pay cuts large enough to save the airline from bankruptcy. At the same moment, the CEO and other executives were slated to receive millions in bonuses for saving the company through those very negotiations. When the truth about the executive bonuses leaked, the unions balked, putting the deal to save the airline in jeopardy. The CEO seemed contrite as he both apologized and explained himself in the following days. A little later, he resigned, perhaps voluntarily, perhaps not, with $1.6 million in severance pay.

We wonder: did the CEO truly repent, or was he merely sorry he got caught? Pastors have too much experience with people who seem both sad and sorry but may be neither. Addicts and congenital liars know how to feign grief to get what they want from their dupes. Such experiences lead us to think repentance is genuine only when someone confesses and shows contrition before being caught. So I know a student has repented when he writes to confess that he cheated on an exam five years ago, then asks forgiveness and declares that he is ready to bear any punishment. But when the latest in the series of fallen politicians, business leaders, or church leaders confess after they get caught, we squint suspiciously. — Daniel M. Doriani, Matthew & 2, ed. Richard D. Phillips, Philip Graham Ryken, and Daniel M. Doriani, *vol. 1, Reformed Expository Commentary* (Phillipsburg, NJ: P&R Publishing, 2008), 47–48.

18. Is repentance an emotion?

When John called Israel to repentance, he did more than summon them to feel sorry for past actions. Repentance may include sorrow that we hurt someone, because sin can cause others pain. But we can sin against someone without hurting them, and we can also inflict pain on others without sinning against them. We sin without causing pain when we envy them or lust after them or plagiarize their ideas. On the other side, dentists, doctors, and physical therapists inflict pain daily, but they need not repent because the pain is attached to their therapy. Teachers and coaches also inflict a kind of pain in order to correct error.

A friendly single woman can also inflict pain on a single man without sin. She smiles at him, calls him by name, and listens attentively when he speaks. The man mistakes her friendliness for romantic interest. Supposing there is a mutual attraction, he gathers his courage and invites her to an event designed to initiate a deeper relationship. She understands his design, and utters the dreaded words, "But I think of you as a friend." The man is crushed and the woman has hurt him, in a way. Yet, if she is friendly and not a flirt, she has not sinned, hence need not repent. So then, sin does hurt others, but repentance is more than sorrow that we hurt someone.

Repentance is also more than sorrow that we hurt ourselves. Sinners are like poor gunslingers. Sins are bullets that can hit others, but sinners also shoot themselves in the foot. As Proverbs says, "The evil deeds of a wicked man ensnare him; the cords of his sin hold him fast" (5:22).

This proverb explains why people commonly show sorrow for a sin after they are caught—the cords of sin do trap the sinner. President Bill Clinton was angry and defiant at first when charged with the sin of an illicit relationship with a White House intern. "I did not have relations with that woman," he thundered, and he questioned the motives of anyone who said he had. A few weeks later, when irrefutable evidence of a relationship with "that woman" became public, Clinton was all remorse. Was he truly penitent? Maybe and maybe not. Who can know the condition of another man's soul? Repentance is more than remorse over shameful behavior, but when a man is caught in a sin, the publicity and the shame can lead to true repentance. The fallen evangelist Jim Bakker seems eventually to have come to true repentance that way. Years after his disgrace, he wrote a striking book entitled I Was Wrong.

Repentance is more than sorrow that we got caught or hurt ourselves or hurt others. The case of Judas makes this clear. Judas betrayed Jesus to death, for reasons we will never fully fathom. The Gospels say he used to steal from the disciples' common purse, that the priests paid him a substantial sum for betraying Jesus, and that Satan entered him (John 12:6; 13:27–30; Matt. 27:1–5). Still, after Jesus' death, Judas was filled with remorse. He tried—and failed—to return the money he gained for betraying Jesus. Later, he took his life. He was sorry for his sin, but instead of taking his sorrow to God, he despaired. He turned inward, not Godward, and his remorse became self-condemnation.

Self-condemnation is not repentance. To wallow in self-recrimination is another form of selfishness. God does not want us to suffocate in our guilt, he wants us to take our guilt to him, that we may find forgiveness and release, peace and renewal. The penitent take their sorrow to the Lord. As he discusses the repentance of certain Christians in Corinth,

Paul says he regrets that his rebuke hurt the church for a little while, yet he is glad because "your sorrow led you to repentance" (2 Cor. 7:8–9). He explains, "You became sorrowful as God intended and so were not harmed in any way by us. Godly sorrow brings repentance that leads to salvation and leaves no regret, but worldly sorrow brings death" (7:9–10).

In worldly sorrow, the sinner feels bad for himself—his pain, his shame, his damaged reputation or relationships. In godly sorrow, the sinner wants to see justice done and wants to restore relationships, first with God, and then with our fellow man (12:11). True repentance looks inward, at one's sinfulness, and outward, at the harm caused to others, and upward, to the Lord. — Daniel M. Doriani, Matthew & 2, ed. Richard D. Phillips, Philip Graham Ryken, and Daniel M. Doriani, *vol. 1, Reformed Expository Commentary* (Phillipsburg, NJ: P&R Publishing, 2008), 49–51.

19. Summary. Summarize what the Bible teaches about repentance.

Question 76 of the Westminster Larger Catechism asks, "What is repentance unto life?" The catechism answers:

Repentance unto life is a saving grace, wrought in the heart of a sinner by the Spirit and the Word of God, whereby, out of the sight and sense, not only of the danger, but also of the filthiness and odiousness of his sins, and upon apprehension of God's mercy in Christ to such as are penitent, he so grieves for and hates his sins, as that he turns from them all to God, purposing and endeavoring constantly to walk with him in all the ways of new obedience.

The pastors and scholars who penned this knew that true repentance is more than shame over misdeeds or sorrow over pain inflicted to self or others. The penitent man grieves that he has offended God. He hates the sin he has committed. The sinner may feel dreadful or numb. He may have caused much damage or little. But the penitent, unlike Judas, refuse to despair. They turn from heinous sin to a gracious God. They know God is merciful; they also know that true repentance entails a constant endeavor to walk with God in obedience. The repentant turn from sin once for all, yet we also turn to Jesus daily for mercy and for healing.

When the catechism calls repentance a grace and fruit of the Spirit, it follows the Scripture that says, "God grants repentance unto life" (Acts 11:18). Unless the Spirit enlightens, we will never see that sin is rebellion against God. The Spirit speaks and convicts, but we listen, agree, forsake our sinful ways and return to the Lord, so that repentance is also our act. In fact, Abraham Kuyper says, "Sacred Scripture refers to conversion almost one hundred and forty times as being an act of man, and only six times as an act of the Holy Ghost." — Daniel M. Doriani, Matthew & 2, ed. Richard D. Phillips, Philip Graham Ryken, and Daniel M. Doriani, *vol. 1, Reformed Expository Commentary* (Phillipsburg, NJ: P&R Publishing, 2008), 51.

20. How can we support one another in prayer this week?

Lesson #2, Matthew 1.18 - 25

Good Questions Have Groups Talking

www.joshhunt.com

Matthew 1.18 - 25

OPEN

Let me ask each of you to share your name, and, how you proposed to your wife (or how your husband proposed to you).

DIG

1. **Overview. It is always a good idea to read the Bible with emotion in mind. As you read, read with emotion. What are the various players feeling in this story? What did God intend us to feel as we read?**

   WHEN MY SON Simeon was three, he liked to look at the moon. We could be walking through our neighborhood on a partially cloudy night or driving along the highway at the break of dawn, and instead of first noticing the colored Christmas lights on the trees or the cool sports car passing on the left, Simeon would spot the moon. "I see the moon!" he'd belt out from his car seat. "I see the moon," he'd say, squeezing my hand as we walked.

   One night at home his gift for observing the obvious was especially memorable. He turned to the window, and there it was again. "Dad, the moon," he said softly and with astonishment, as if he had never seen it before. "I know, Simeon," I replied mildly and with less astonishment. I added playfully, "Do you think you can touch it?" Without hesitation he turned to the window, climbed up the arm of a chair, crossed over onto the windowsill, and reached his right hand up to the sky. He was only 384,403 kilometers shy of it. Discouraged but not dissuaded, he jumped down and ran to the front room, once again finding the moon. "There's another one," he yelled. Then he backed up. He ran. He leapt. He reached. This time I swear he almost touched it.

To Simeon the moon's movements were mysterious, its light lovely, and its texture close enough to touch. Sometimes when we come to passages like Matthew's condensed Christmas story, we don't come with that childlike curiosity and wonder—looking at the everyday with awe, perceiving the familiar as fascinating. But we should. We should become like little children, which Jesus said is the only way to get into the kingdom. — Douglas Sean O'Donnell, *Matthew: All Authority in Heaven and on Earth,* ed. R. Kent Hughes, *Preaching the Word* (Wheaton, IL: Crossway, 2013), 39.

2.   Read between the lines. Best you can tell, how was the process of getting engaged and married different back in the day? If you have a study Bible, it likely has a note on this.

The Jews of first-century Palestine saw marriage as a joining of two families. And because the stakes were so high, they never would have entrusted such an important decision to the whims of teenage emotions. As in many cultures, both past and present, first-century Hebrew parents arranged the marriages of their sons and daughters. According to rabbinical law, this could take place sometime after the age of consent: twelve for girls, thirteen for boys. While the children weren't given the final word in the matter, their personal desires were usually taken into account.

Once the decision was made to pursue the match, the fathers discussed every detail of the arrangement and prepared a legal contract, which would be read during the marriage ceremony. Vows were made, tokens were exchanged, and the families celebrated. At the conclusion of the ceremony, the boy and girl would enter the betrothal period, which could be no less than one month, but typically lasted one year. — Charles R. Swindoll, *Jesus: The Greatest Life of All* (Nashville: Thomas Nelson, 2011).

3. What exactly is the relationship between Mary and Joseph at this point?

During the betrothal period, the newly married couple was husband and wife in every respect except that they were to live with their respective families and refrain from sex. This interval between the vows and the home-taking served several purposes. First, it gave the groom time to prepare the couple's new home, usually a one-room addition to his parents' house. Second, it gave the bride time to complete several purification rituals and to demonstrate that she was sexually pure. Proof of paternity was of supreme importance in Jewish law, so a divorced woman or widow had to wait no fewer than ninety days in order to prove she did not carry her former husband's child. Third, unlike many other cultures, Jews didn't expect a young girl to leave her family one morning and lie in the bed of a stranger that night. The betrothal period gave the husband and wife plenty of time to bond under the strict supervision of their families before coming together as a couple. Though they lived apart, the community viewed the couple as married. To end the marriage during the betrothal period required an official divorce decree. And if either of them engaged in sex with someone else, it was considered adultery, which could carry the penalty of death by stoning.

When the bride had completed her purification and the groom was ready to receive her, the groom and his wedding party would arrive at her house, where he called for his bride to join him. This was the home-taking. The wedding party would lift the couple into the air and carry them to their new home, where the families and guests would celebrate the nuptials for as many as seven days.

It was during the betrothal period—between the vows and the home-taking—that Jesus was conceived by the Holy Spirit in Mary's womb. — Charles R. Swindoll, *Jesus: The Greatest Life of All* (Nashville: Thomas Nelson, 2011).

4. **Liberal scholars question the story of the virgin birth. Assuming you believe in the virgin birth, how would you articulate your belief to someone who did not believe in the virgin birth?**

In referring to Mary, both Luke and Matthew employ the Greek term parthenos, which means "virgin." Some have argued that this merely points to a girl who is young and eligible for marriage, not necessarily one untouched by a man. But the ancient Greeks took this term quite literally. For instance, Artemis, the goddess whose temple in Ephesus is considered one of the seven ancient wonders of the world, was emphatically virginal. She was thought to protect chaste young men and women, and she symbolized the cultic power of virginity, representing "young and budding life and strict innocence." Consequently, a young, unmarried woman was called a parthenos. To be anything other than a virgin before her wedding would have been unthinkable! — Charles R. Swindoll, *Jesus: The Greatest Life of All* (Nashville: Thomas Nelson, 2011).

5. **By the way, another phrase often gets confused with the phrase, "virgin birth," and that is "Immaculate Conception." What is the difference between these two terms? What is the Immaculate Conception?**

The idea that the Virgin Mary did not have original sin at her conception nor did she acquire elements of original sin in the development of her life, whereas all other human beings have original sin from their conception due to the fall of Adam. The immaculate conception is an article of faith for Roman Catholics, who believe that Mary, as the Mother of God, did not have original sin because of the direct intervention of God. Mary was immaculate as a divine privilege. The Roman Catholic Church considers the doctrine of the immaculate conception of the Virgin Mary to be part of apostolic teaching related to both the Bible and tradition. It holds that the doctrine is referred to, at least implicitly, in Genesis 3:15, which indicates a woman who will battle Satan. The woman ultimately wins the battle. Pope Pius IX said that this section of the Bible foretells the immaculate conception. He described his view in "Ineffabilis Deus." — Walter A. Elwell, *Evangelical Dictionary of Theology: Second Edition* (Grand Rapids, MI: Baker Academic, 2001), 595–596.

6. While we are on the subject of Catholic theology, what do you know about the doctrine of the perpetual virginity of Mary?

Based on Isaiah 7:14, Matthew 1:18, and Luke 1:26 (cf. Gal. 4:4) both Protestants and Catholics believe that Jesus was conceived of a virgin. This has been universally taught in the Catholic church as a de fide dogma of the faith. Since all orthodox non-Catholic Christians agree we will not discuss Mary's initial virgin state further, given that our purpose in this section is to focus on the differences between Catholic and Protestant doctrine.

Catholics also believe, contrary to Protestants, that Jesus was also born in a way that left Mary a virgin. Ott puts it this way: "Mary bore her son without any violation of her virginal integrity."4 This is considered an official doctrine of Catholicism on the grounds of general proclamation. How this happened, however, is not a matter of Catholic dogma. Generally, traditional Catholic scholarship held that "Mary gave birth in miraculous fashion without opening of the womb and injury to the hymen, and consequently also without pains."

Admitting that Mary's virginity was retained during Christ's birth has scant support in Scripture. Catholic scholars often point to the fact that "Holy Writ attests Mary's active role in the act of birth (Mt. 1, 25; Luke 2, 7): 'She brought forth' . . . , which does not seem to indicate a miraculous process."

Catholic dogma also states that "after the birth of Jesus Mary remained a Virgin (De fide)." Hence, the title "perpetual virginity" is attributed to Mary. Roman Catholics defend this belief from both Scripture and tradition. — Norman L. Geisler and Ralph E. MacKenzie, *Roman Catholics and Evangelicals: Agreements and Differences* (Grand Rapids, MI: Baker Books, 1995), 300.

7. One more. Catholica also believe in the sinlessness of Mary. What do they base this on? How would you respond to such a teaching?

Not only was Mary conceived without original sin but, according to Catholic teaching, "from her conception Mary was free from all motions of concupiscence." And "in consequence of a special privilege of grace from God, Mary was free from every personal sin during her whole life." The Council of Trent declared that "no justified person can for his whole life avoid all sins, even venial sins, except on the ground of a special privilege from God such as the Church holds was given to the Blessed Virgin."

CATHOLIC DEFENSE OF THE SINLESSNESS OF MARY

According to Catholic dogma, Mary had neither the tendency to sin nor did she ever actually sin during her entire life. Catholics use both Scripture and tradition to support this view.

ARGUMENT FROM SCRIPTURE

According to Roman Catholic teaching, "Mary's sinlessness may be deduced from the text: Luke 1:28: 'Hail, full of grace!' since personal moral defects are irreconcilable with fullness of grace." Grace is taken here to be both extensive and preventative.

ARGUMENT FROM TRADITION

The house of church fathers was divided on Mary's sinlessness. Nonetheless, Roman Catholic scholars point with pride to the fact that "the Latin Patristic authors unanimously teach the doctrine of the sinlessness of Mary." Again, this is far short of the "unanimous consent" of all church fathers, which the Council of Trent claimed for dogma.

PROTESTANT RESPONSE TO THE SINLESSNESS OF MARY

The Bible does not support the sinlessness of Mary. To the contrary, it affirms her sinfulness. Speaking as a sinner, Mary said, "my spirit rejoices in God my savior" (Luke 1:46). An examination of the text used to prove Mary's sinlessness reveals the lack of any real support for such a doctrine. Contrary to Scotus's solution of her being prevented from needing to be saved from sin, she was confessing her present need (after her conception) of a Savior. Indeed, she even presented an offering to the Jewish priest arising out of her sinful condition (Luke 2:22–24) which was required by law (Lev. 12). This would not have been necessary if she were sinless. — Norman L. Geisler and Ralph E. MacKenzie, *Roman Catholics and Evangelicals: Agreements and Differences* (Grand Rapids, MI: Baker Books, 1995), 309–310.

8. I'd like for us to talk about Joseph a bit. What do you know about Joseph?

Matthew describes Jesus' earthly father as a craftsman (Matthew 13:55). A small-town carpenter, he lives in Nazareth: a single-camel map dot on the edge of boredom. Is he the right choice? Doesn't God have better options? An eloquent priest from Jerusalem or a scholar from the Pharisees?

Why Joseph? A major part of the answer lies in his reputation: he gives it up for Jesus. "Then Joseph [Mary's] husband, being a just man, and not wanting to make her a public example, was minded to put her away secretly" (Matthew 1:19).

With the phrase "a just man," Matthew recognizes the status of Joseph. Nazareth viewed him as we might view an elder, deacon, or Bible class teacher. Joseph likely took pride in his standing, but Mary's announcement jeopardized it. I'm pregnant.

Now what? His fiancée is blemished, tainted . . . he is righteous, godly. On the one hand, he has the law. On the other hand, he has his love. The law says, stone her. Love says, forgive her. Joseph is caught in the middle.

Then comes the angel. Mary's growing belly gives no cause for concern, but reason to rejoice. "She carries the Son of

God in her womb," the angel announces. But who would believe it?

A bead of sweat forms beneath Joseph's beard. He faces a dilemma. Make up a lie and preserve his place in the community, or tell the truth and kiss his reputation good-bye. He makes his decision. "Joseph . . . took to him his wife, and did not know her till she had brought forth her firstborn Son" (Matthew 1:24–25).

Joseph swapped his Torah studies for a pregnant fiancée and an illegitimate son and made the big decision of discipleship. He placed God's plan ahead of his own. — Max Lucado, *In the Manger: 25 Inspirational Selections for Advent* (Nashville: Thomas Nelson, 2012).

9. What do you admire about Joseph from verse 19? What is the example and application for us?

What a remarkable man! What a tactful stand he took! He had every reason to believe that Mary had been unfaithful. And to marry an unfaithful woman who clung to such an outlandish story would have been irresponsible. Nevertheless, Joseph planned to deal with her mercifully. He would pursue a quiet divorce. He could get on with his life. She could remain with her family, who would care for Mary and the child. It was a logical, wise decision. — Charles R. Swindoll, *Jesus: The Greatest Life of All* (Nashville: Thomas Nelson, 2011).

10. Try to imagine how Joseph felt. What does his example teach us about what we can expect as we follow God?

Three months pass before Joseph receives word that she has returned. Upon first glance, he notices a slight bulge in her outer garment. He doesn't know much, only that life has suddenly become very complicated. Here's how I imagine Joseph recalling his experience:

After describing a most unusual story, Mary revealed that she was pregnant.

The words hit my chest like a boulder. I sat stunned as she continued with a preposterous, blasphemous story about conceiving the Messiah and the invisible God behaving in a manner that seemed to me like the deviant gods of Rome. A wave of questions flooded my mind. Who was the father? Was she taken advantage of, or did she consent? How could I have been so wrong about someone I knew so well? Is she insane? Is she in love with him? Does she not love me? Why would she do this?

I looked across the table at Mary to find her gazing at me with obvious compassion, which outraged me. Was her delusion so complete as to believe what she said? Or, worse, her deceit so profound as to feign concern for the lives she destroyed? The room began to spin and I felt my stomach rebel. I had to get outside.

I nearly tore the door off its hinges, ran into the night, and didn't stop until I stood on the ridge outside Nazareth. Exhausted, I sank to my knees then sat for hours in the darkness, staring across the plain and into the night sky. When I was a child, I had found comfort in the vast expanse of stars, a symbol of God's power, permanence, and unchangeable character. So, I found the appearance of a new light—a bright dot high above the horizon—a little unsettling. But my anguish would allow no other thoughts for very long before the utter absurdity of my circumstances overtook me. Each time I recovered, a new dimension of this tragedy invaded my mind and brought with it another spasm of sobs.

As the horizon turned light blue and then pink, I made my way home. My parents, though grieved and bewildered by the turn of events, advised me to delay making any decision regarding Mary. It was wise advice. One moment I wanted to rush to her side, the next I wanted to wash my hands of her. But one constant remained through all of my pain and confusion: an unrelenting love for Mary. — Charles R. Swindoll, *Jesus: The Greatest Life of All* (Nashville: Thomas Nelson, 2011).

11. What choices did Joseph have?

According to Jewish law, Joseph had the right to demand a public stoning, which would not only salve his wounded honor, but would also clear his name in the community. But he was too honorable for that. — Charles R. Swindoll, *Jesus: The Greatest Life of All* (Nashville: Thomas Nelson, 2011).

12. Would it have been sinful for Joseph to expose Mary's pregnancy publicly?

Being a just man, he could not simply disregard God's Law (see Deuteronomy 22:23–27), and to marry Mary would have been to do just that. It would have been to overlook an offense that God's Word says should not be overlooked. In fact, it would have been to admit guilt when he was not guilty. In a sense, it would be to lie—"Yes, it's my child; shame on us."

I envision the weight of this decision in this way. On one shoulder Joseph has the righteous requirements of God's Law whispering in his ear, "You have to expose her error. This sin cannot go unpunished." On the other shoulder is the compassion and mercy of God's Law (cf. 23:23). (And note here that it's not a devil and an angel on his shoulders; these are two angels, if you will; two angels wrestling with his heart.) Compassion counsels him, "Joseph, a private divorce is the way to proceed. Dismiss her quietly. In this way you show both the justice and the love of God." — Douglas Sean O'Donnell, *Matthew: All Authority in Heaven and on Earth*, ed. R. Kent Hughes, *Preaching the Word* (Wheaton, IL: Crossway, 2013), 41.

13. Think of the rest of Joseph and Mary's life. How did this story impact the rest of the story for them? Again, what is the lesson for us? What do we learn about following God from this story?

Joseph and Mary would have to rest confidently in the truth of their innocence and find contentment in that. No one would believe the truth no matter how hard they tried to convince them. Whispers and snickering and jokes and scorn would be their closest and most enduring companions. This would either draw them together, or it would become a wedge. They would either seek opposite corners of the house or turn toward each other for strength. Stop and think. Everything hinged on their commitment to each other.

If the couple remains committed, their marriage will endure the strangest circumstances. No one outside the couple may understand (including their parents), and the married pair may be left with no external support, but if they remain committed to each other and the covenant they made with God, the marriage will survive. In fact, the intimacy may even grow sweeter as the two share a perspective that no one else on earth would appreciate.

You may be faced with an unusual set of circumstances that challenges your marriage from the outside. Having been in ministry for more than four decades, I've helped a lot of folks going through terrible times. So I know how difficult life can be when dealing with problems in a marriage. Nevertheless, in all these years I've never seen one marriage get worse when the partners redouble their commitment to each other. The problems may not go away, but the marriage only gets stronger. — Charles R. Swindoll, *Marriage: From Surviving to Thriving* (Nashville: Thomas Nelson, 2006).

14. Jesus was given two names. What are they? Why do you think He was given two names? What does each name mean?

Matthew says God has been orchestrating the needed deliverance. Since the Lord often uses names to reveal his purposes, he gives baby Jesus more than one name; no single name could describe all that he is. The baby is called both Jesus and Immanuel. Jesus means "God saves"; the name is given "because he will save his people from their sins" (Matt. 1:21).

Immanuel means "God with us." The name Immanuel, says Matthew, fulfills a prophecy. — Daniel M. Doriani, Matthew & 2, ed. Richard D. Phillips, Philip Graham Ryken, and

Daniel M. Doriani, vol. 1, *Reformed Expository Commentary* (Phillipsburg, NJ: P&R Publishing, 2008), 15–16.

15. Can you think of any other names of Jesus?

Names, Appellations, and Titles of: Adam, 1 Cor. 15:45. Advocate, 1 John 2:1. Almighty, Rev. 1:8. Alpha and Omega, Rev. 1:8. Amen, Rev. 3:14. Angel, Gen. 48:16; Ex. 23:20, 21. Angel of his presence, Isa. 63:9. Anointed, Psa. 2:2. Apostle, Heb. 3:1. Arm of the Lord, Isa. 51:9, 10. Author and perfecter of our faith, Heb. 12:2. Beginning and end of the creation of God, Rev. 3:14; 22:13. Beloved, Eph. 1:6. Bishop, 1 Pet. 2:25. Blessed and only Potentate, 1 Tim. 6:15. Branch, Jer. 23:5; Zech. 3:8. Bread of life, John 6:48. Bridegroom, Matt. 9:15. Bright and morning star, Rev. 22:16. Brightness of the Father's glory, Heb. 1:3. Captain of the Lord's army, Josh. 5:14. Captain of salvation, Heb. 2:10. Carpenter, Mark 6:3. Carpenter's son, Matt. 13:55. Chief Shepherd, 1 Pet. 5:4. Chief corner stone, 1 Pet. 2:6. Outstanding among ten thousand, Song 5:10. Child, Isa. 9:6; Luke 2:27, 43. Chosen of God, 1 Pet. 2:4. Christ, Matt. 1:16; Luke 9:20. The Christ, Matt. 16:20; Mark 14:61. Christ, a King, Luke 23:2. Christ Jesus, Acts 19:4; Rom. 3:24; 8:1; 1 Cor. 1:2; 1 Cor. 1:30; Heb. 3:1; 1 Pet. 5:10, 14. Christ Jesus our Lord, 1 Tim. 1:12; Rom. 8:39. Christ of God, Luke 9:20. Christ, the chosen of God, Luke 23:35. Christ the Lord, Luke 2:11; Christ the power of God, 1 Cor. 1:24. Christ the wisdom of God, 1 Cor. 1:24. Christ, the Son of God, Acts 9:20. Christ, Son of the Blessed, Mark 14:61. Commander, Isa. 55:4. Consolation of Israel, Luke 2:25. Corner stone, Eph. 2:20. Counselor, Isa. 9:6. Covenant of the people, Isa. 42:6. David, Jer. 30:9. Daysman, Job 9:33. Dayspring, Luke 1:78. Day star, 2 Pet. 1:19. Deliverer, Rom. 11:26. Desire of all nations, Hag. 2:7. Door, John 10:7. Elect, Isa. 42:1. Emmanuel, Isa. 7:14. Ensign, Isa. 11:10. Eternal life, 1 John 5:20. Everlasting Father, Isa. 9:6. Faithful and True, Rev. 19:11. Faithful witness, Rev. 1:5. Faithful and true witness, Rev. 3:14. Finisher of faith, Heb. 12:2. First and last, Rev. 1:17; 2:8; 22:13. First begotten, Heb. 1:6. First begotten of the dead, Rev. 1:5. Firstborn, Psa. 89:27. Foundation, Isa. 28:16. Fountain, Zech. 13:1. Forerunner, Heb. 6:20. Friend of sinners, Matt. 11:19. Gift of God, John 4:10. Glory of Israel,

Luke 2:32. God, John 1:1. God blessed for ever, Rom. 9:5. God manifest in the flesh, 1 Tim. 3:16. God of Israel, the Savior, Isa. 45:15. God of the whole earth, Isa. 54:5. God our Savior, 1 Tim. 2:3. God's dear Son, Col. 1:13. God with us, Matt. 1:23. Good Master, Matt. 19:16. Governor, Matt. 2:6. Great shepherd of the sheep, Heb. 13:20. Head of the church, Eph. 5:23. Heir of all things, Heb. 1:2. High priest, Heb. 4:14. Head of every man, 1 Cor. 11:3. Head of the church, Col. 1:18. Head of the corner, Matt. 21:42. Holy child Jesus, Acts 4:30. Holy one, Psa. 16:10; Acts 3:14. Holy one of God, Mark 1:24. Holy one of Israel, Isa. 41:14; 54:5. Holy thing, Luke 1:35. Hope [our], 1 Tim. 1:1. Horn of salvation, Luke 1:69. I Am, John 8:58. Image of God, Heb. 1:3. Israel, Isa. 49:3. Jehovah, Isa. 40:3. Jehovah's fellow, Zech. 13:7. Jesus, Matt. 1:21. Jesus Christ, Matt. 1:1; John 1:17; 17:3; Acts 2:38; 4:10; 9:34; 10:36; 16:18; Rom. 1:1, 3, 6; 2:16; 5:15, 17; 6:3; 1 Cor. 1:1, 4; 1 Cor. 2:2; 2 Cor. 1:19; 4:6; 13:5; Gal. 2:16; Phil. 1:8; 2:11; 1 Tim. 1:15; Heb. 13:8; 1 John 1:7; 2:1. Jesus Christ our Lord, Rom. 1:3; 6:11, 23; 1 Cor. 1:9; 7:25. Jesus Christ our Savior, Tit. 3:6. Jesus of Nazareth, Mark 1:24; Luke 24:19. Jesus of Nazareth, King of the Jews, John 19:19. Jesus, the King of the Jews, Matt. 27:37. Jesus, the Son of God, Heb. 4:14. Jesus, the Son of Joseph, John 6:42. Judge, Acts 10:42. Just man, Matt. 27:19. Just one, Acts 3:14; 7:52; 22:14. Just person, Matt. 27:24. King, Matt. 21:5. King of Israel, John 1:49. King of the Jews, Matt. 2:2. King of saints, Rev. 15:3. King of kings, 1 Tim. 6:15; Rev. 17:14. King of glory, Psa. 24:7–10. King of Zion, Matt. 21:5. King over all the earth, Zech. 14:9. Lamb, Rev. 5:6, 8; 6:16; 7:9, 10, 17; 12:11; 13:8, 11; 14:1, 4; 15:3; 17:14; 19:7, 9; 21:9, 14, 22, 23, 27. Lamb of God, John 1:29. Lawgiver, Isa. 33:22. Leader, Isa. 55:4. Life, John 14:6. Light, John 8:12. Light, everlasting, Isa. 60:20. Light of the world, John 8:12. Light to the Gentiles, Isa. 42:6. Light, true, John 1:9. Living bread, John 6:51. Living stone, 1 Pet. 2:4. Lion of the tribe of Judah, Rev. 5:5. Lord, Rom. 1:3. Lord of lords, Rev. 17:14; 19:16. Lord of all, Acts 10:36. Lord our righteousness, Jer. 23:6. Lord God Almighty, Rev. 15:3. Lord from heaven, 1 Cor. 15:47. Lord and Savior Jesus Christ, 2 Pet. 1:11; 3:18. Lord Christ, Col. 3:24. Lord Jesus, Acts 7:59; Col. 3:17; 1 Thess. 4:2. Lord Jesus Christ, Acts 11:17; 16:31; 20:21; Rom. 5:1, 11; 13:14. Lord Jesus Christ our Savior, Tit. 1:4. Lord of glory, Jas. 2:1. Lord of Armies, Isa. 44:6. Lord, mighty in battle, Psa. 24:8. Lord of the dead and living, Rom. 14:9. Lord of the sabbath, Mark 2:28. Lord over all, Rom. 10:12. Lord's Christ, Luke 2:26. Lord, strong and mighty, Psa. 24:8. Lord, the, our righteousness, Jer. 23:6. Lord, your holy one, Isa. 43:15. Lord, your redeemer, Isa. 43:14. Man Christ Jesus, 1 Tim. 2:5. One of sorrows, Isa. 53:3. Master, Matt. 23:8. Mediator, 1 Tim. 2:5. Messenger of the covenant, Mal. 3:1. Messiah, John 1:41. Messiah the Prince, Dan. 9:25. Mighty God, Isa. 9:6. Mighty one of Israel, Isa. 30:29. Mighty one of Jacob, Isa. 49:26. Mighty to save, Isa. 63:1. Minister of the sanctuary, Heb. 8:2. Morning star, Rev. 22:16. Most holy, Dan. 9:24. Most mighty, Psa. 45:3. Nazarene, Matt. 2:23. Offspring of David, Rev. 22:16. Only begotten, John 1:14. Only begotten of the Father, John 1:14. Only begotten son, John 1:18. Only wise God, our Savior, Jude 25. Passover, 1 Cor. 5:7. Plant of renown, Ezek. 34:29. Potentate, 1 Tim. 6:15. Power of God, 1 Cor. 1:24. Physician, Matt. 9:12. Precious corner stone, Isa. 28:16. Priest, Heb. 7:17. Prince, Acts 5:31. Prince of life, Acts 3:15. Prince of peace, Isa. 9:6. Prince of the kings of the earth, Rev. 1:5. Prophet, Deut. 18:15, 18; Matt. 21:11; Luke 24:19. Propitiation, 1 John 2:2. Rabbi, John 1:49. Rabboni, John 20:16. Ransom, 1 Tim. 2:6. Redeemer, Isa. 59:20. Resurrection and life, John 11:25. Redemption, 1 Cor. 1:30. Righteous branch, Jer. 23:5. Righteous judge, 2 Tim. 4:8. Righteous servant, Isa. 53:11. Righteousness, 1 Cor. 1:30. Rock, 1 Cor. 10:4. Rock of offence, 1 Pet. 2:8. Root of David, Rev. 5:5; 22:16. Root of Jesse, Isa. 11:10. Rose of Sharon, Song 2:1. Ruler in Israel, Mic. 5:2. Salvation, Luke 2:30. Sanctification, 1 Cor. 1:30. Sanctuary, Isa. 8:14. Savior, Luke 2:11. Savior, Jesus Christ, 2 Tim. 1:10; Tit. 2:13; 2 Pet. 1:1. Savior of the body, Eph. 5:23. Savior of the world, 1 John 4:14. Scepter, Num. 24:17. Second Adam, 1 Cor. 15:47. Seed of David, 2 Tim. 2:8. Seed of the woman, Gen. 3:15. Servant, Isa. 42:1. Servant of rulers, Isa. 49:7. Shepherd, Mark 14:27. Shepherd and bishop of souls, 1 Pet. 2:25. Shepherd, chief, 1 Pet. 5:4. Shepherd, good, John 10:11. Shepherd, great, Heb. 13:20. Shepherd of Israel, Psa. 80:1. Shiloh, Gen. 49:10. Son of the Father, 2 John 3. Son of God, see SON OF GOD. Son of Man, see SON OF MAN. Son of the blessed, Mark 14:61. Son of the highest, Luke 1:32. Son of David, Matt. 9:27. Star,

Num. 24:17. Sun of righteousness, Mal. 4:2. Surety, Heb. 7:22. Stone, Matt. 21:42. Stone of stumbling, 1 Pet. 2:8. Sure foundation, Isa. 28:16. Teacher, John 3:2. True God, 1 John 5:20. True vine, John 15:1. Truth, John 14:6. Unspeakable gift, 2 Cor. 9:15. Very Christ, Acts 9:22. Vine, John 15:1. Way, John 14:6. Which is, which was, which is to come, Rev. 1:4. Wisdom, Prov. 8:12. Wisdom of God, 1 Cor. 1:24. Witness, Isa. 55:4; Rev. 1:5. Wonderful, Isa. 9:6. Word, John 1:1. Word of God, Rev. 19:13. Word of life, 1 John 1:1. Those who use his name must depart from evil, 2 Tim. 2:19.

— James Swanson and Orville Nave, *New Nave's Topical Bible* (Oak Harbor: Logos Research Systems, 1994).

16. How could familiarizing ourselves with some of the names of Jesus help our walk with God?

Joy, peace, and power—these are only some of the gifts promised to those who trust in the name of the Lord. Praying the Names of Jesus will lead readers into a richer and more rewarding relationship with Christ by helping them to understand and to pray his names on a daily basis. They will also begin to see how each of his names holds within it a promise: to be our Teacher, Healer, Friend, and Lord — to be God-with-Us no matter the circumstances. — Ann Spangler, *Immanuel: A Daily Guide to Reclaiming the True Meaning of Christmas* (Grand Rapids, MI: Zondervan, 2009).

17. Let's think of one of the names of Jesus as an example: comforter. How could knowing the name comforter make a difference in our lives? Be very practical.

God is always your Comforter, and there is never a time when you are alone or abandoned. One of the names of Jesus is Comforter. When Jesus left this earth and returned to heaven, He sent the Holy Spirit to comfort us.

Have you ever stopped to consider, though, when you most appreciate God's role as Comforter? You are keenly aware of His gentle encouragement and refreshment after times of great personal pain or affliction. In fact, sometimes God allows you to go through such trials so that you will learn to seek His comfort.

In John Bunyan's book, The Pilgrim's Progress, the main character, Christian, realizes this truth after he has passed through the Valley of the Shadow of Death:

> But now the day was dawning. Viewing the eastern hills, Christian said to himself, "God has turned the shadows of death into the morning." Looking back over the way he had come, he wondered how the Lord had gotten him through.
>
> He remembered the verse: "He reveals the deep things of darkness and brings deep shadows into the light." He was deeply moved when he saw all the dangers from which he had been delivered … Now he could see his way, and he went on past them all, saying, "His candle shines on my head, and by His light I go through darkness."

God knows the way through the trickiest and most discouraging circumstances. Then you have the joy of looking back on the path you have traveled during the past year and thanking Him for restoring you to safety and peace. — Charles F. Stanley, Seeking His Face (Nashville, TN: Thomas Nelson Publishers, 2002), 352.

18. Verse 23. What do we learn about God from this verse?

God's treatment for insignificance won't lead you to a bar or dating service, a spouse or social club. God's ultimate cure for the common life takes you to a manger. The babe of Bethlehem. Immanuel. Remember the promise of the angel? "'Behold, the virgin shall be with child, and bear a Son, and they shall call His name Immanuel,' which is translated, 'God with us'" (Matt. 1:23 NKJV).

Immanuel. The name appears in the same Hebrew form as it did two thousand years ago. "Immanu" means "with us." "El" refers to Elohim, or God. Not an "above us God" or a "somewhere in the neighborhood God." He came as the "with us God." God with us.

Not "God with the rich" or "God with the religious." But God with us. All of us. Russians, Germans, Buddhists, Mormons, truckdrivers and taxi drivers, librarians. God with us. — *Cure for the Common Life* / Max Lucado, *Grace for the Moment® Volume Ii: More Inspirational Thoughts for Each Day of the Year* (Nashville: Thomas Nelson, 2006).

19. Verse 23. God is with us. What difference does it make? What does it mean to our day-to-day lives?

The white space between Bible verses is fertile soil for questions. One can hardly read Scripture without whispering, "I wonder ..."

"I wonder if Eve ever ate any more fruit."

"I wonder if Noah slept well during storms." ...

But in our wonderings, there is one question we never need to ask. Does God care? Do we matter to God? Does he still love his children?

Through the small face of the stable-born baby, he says yes.

Yes, your sins are forgiven.

Yes, your name is written in heaven....

And yes, God has entered your world. Immanuel. God is with us. — *He Still Moves Stones* / Max Lucado and Terri A. Gibbs, *Grace for the Moment: Inspirational Thoughts for Each Day of the Year* (Nashville, TN: J. Countryman, 2000), 128.

20. What do you want to recall from today's conversation?

21. How can we support on another in prayer this week?

Lesson #3, Matthew 2.1 - 12
Good Questions Have Groups Talking
www.joshhunt.com

Email your people and ask them to read over Matthew 2. You might ask them to read any notes they have in study Bibles, as well as commentaries they can find online. If you have people who like to study and do research, you might ask a different one to do some reading on each of the following:

- The wise men

- The star

- Herod

- The gifts (gold, frankincense and myrrh)

- Where was Jesus from? Bethlehem? Egypt? Nazareth?

Matthew 2.1 - 12

OPEN

Let me ask each of you to share your name, and, what is the last gift you have or received?

DIG

1. Matthew 2.1 – 12. What do we learn about God from this passage?

The note of fulfilment is very prominent in this story. The king who was to sit on David's throne for ever would be born in Bethlehem. The shepherd who would care for Israel for ever would be born in Bethlehem. That is what Micah had predicted seven centuries beforehand—an example of the way in which the New Testament fulfils the Old even to the smallest detail. It shows, too, that God's overarching plan of salvation spans the millennia. This is already the third example of promise and fulfilment that Matthew has brought before his readers. There will be many others. It is an essential quality in God as the Bible depicts him: he keeps his promises. — Michael Green, *The Message of Matthew: The Kingdom of Heaven, The Bible Speaks Today* (Leicester, England; Downers Grove, IL: InterVarsity Press, 2001), 67.

2. What do we learn about being godly? We always want to read the Bible with a look-out for application. What is the application for us?

From a young age, we are wired to make promises and expect promises from others. "I promise" is a vow routinely on the lips of children and adults, and "But you promised!" can be the greatest of constraints on human behavior. Yet in words and actions human beings often let down those to whom they have made promises. We often promise more than we can deliver. According to Matthew, God's promises to Israel are now being fully realized and fulfilled in Jesus the Messiah. As Paul corroborates in 2 Corinthians 1:20, "No matter how many promises God has made, they are 'Yes' in Christ." — Jeannine K. Brown, Matthew, ed. Mark L. Strauss and John H. Walton, *Teach the Text Commentary Series* (Grand Rapids, MI: Baker Books, 2015), 27.

3. Matthew 2.1. What do you know about Herod?

Jesus was born in the days when Herod was king of Judaea. Standing only four feet four inches tall, Herod was a short man who wanted to prove he was a big guy. He became a master builder, erecting palaces, fortresses, and entire cities. He built Masada, Herod's royal citadel; aqueducts; and remodeled the temple in Jerusalem. He made monuments of great grandeur to his name and to his legacy. However, he was also a cruel and vicious individual who murdered his wife and three sons in the same evening, prompting Caesar Augustus to say, "It is safer to be Herod's pig than his son."

Well into his seventies, and realizing no one would mourn his death, Herod ordered the arrest of one hundred of the leading men of Jerusalem. He put them in prison and demanded that the moment he died, those hundred men were to be killed instantly. In his reasoning, he stated, "If the city won't mourn for me, let it mourn for those who die with me." The men were arrested, and Herod eventually died, but his final order was never carried out.

Herod was actually an Edomite, and not a Jew at all. The Edomites were the descendants of Esau. Jacob and Esau, who began warring in their mother's womb, continued their battle throughout history. This war began between the sons of Jacob—Israel versus the sons of Esau—the Edomites. And here we find them still at war in Matthew chapter 2 as a son of Esau, Herod, is trying to slaughter a Son of Jacob, Jesus.

How did Herod become king? He was a conniver who gained political influence through his dealings with Mark Antony of Cleopatra fame. A powerful person in Rome at that time, Mark Antony appointed Herod king of Judaea. This enabled Herod to become the potentate of Judaea, although in actuality, he was a puppet of Rome. It was during this period when Herod was king that the wise men, or magi, came from the East.

Jon Courson, Jon Courson's Application Commentary (Nashville, TN: Thomas Nelson, 2003), 8.

4. Locate Bethlehem on a map. You might also do a search for Bethlehem in the Old Testament. Is Bethlehem still around?

It was in Bethlehem that Jesus was born. Bethlehem was quite a little town six miles to the south of Jerusalem. In the olden days it had been called Ephrath or Ephratah. The name Bethlehem means The House of Bread, and Bethlehem stood in a fertile countryside, which made its name a fitting name. It stood high up on a grey limestone ridge more than two thousand five hundred feet in height. The ridge had a summit at each end, and a hollow like a saddle between them. So, from its position, Bethlehem looked like a town set in an amphitheatre of hills.

Bethlehem had a long history. It was there that Jacob had buried Rachel, and had set up a pillar of memory beside her grave (Gen 48:7; Gen 35:20). It was there that Ruth had lived when she married Boaz (Ru 1:22), and from Bethlehem Ruth could see the land of Moab, her native land, across the Jordan valley. But above all Bethlehem was the home and the city of David (1 Sam 16:1; 1 Sam 17:12; 1 Sam 20:6); and it was for the water of the well of Bethlehem that David longed when he was a hunted fugitive upon the hills (2 Sam 23:14-15). In later days we read that Rehoboam fortified the town of Bethlehem (2 Chr 11:6). But in the history of Israel, and to the minds of the people, Bethlehem was uniquely the city of David. It was from the line of David that God was to send the great deliverer of his people. As the prophet Micah had it: "O Bethlehem Ephratah, who are little to be among the clans of Judah, from you shall come forth for me one who is to be ruler in Israel, whose origin is from old, from ancient days" (Mic 5:2).

It was in Bethlehem, David's city, that the Jews expected great David's greater Son to be born; it was there that they expected God's Anointed One to come into the world. And it was so. — *Barclay's Daily Study Bible (NT).*

5. Verse 2. Perhaps you have a study Bible with a note. What do we know about this star?

What about the star that seems to have guided them to that home? Many have attempted to explain it as an astronomical phenomenon. The earliest theorists viewed it as a comet. Such was the view of the great church father Origen of Alexandria. Later, Johannes Kepler, the father of modern astronomy, explained it as the conjunction of Jupiter and Saturn in the constellation of Pisces in the year 7 B.C. This view has been elaborated in various ways and is probably the favorite explanation of astronomers today.

More than likely, however, the "star" was a miraculous phenomenon, possibly an appearance of the Shekinah glory that had accompanied the people of Israel in their desert wanderings, signifying God's presence with them. Only something like the Shekinah could have led the wise men over the desert to Jerusalem, reappeared after their meeting with King Herod, guided them to Bethlehem, and then "stopped over the place where the child was" (v. 9), which is what the most straightforward reading of the story seems to indicate.

The Bible shows little interest in these details. The fact that so little information of this kind is given shows that Matthew was not interested in how many wise men there were, the length of their journey, or the star. Rather, he was interested in the fact that from the very beginning of this story, Gentiles came to worship the Jewish Messiah. He was also interested in the significance of the gifts they bore. — James Montgomery Boice, *The Gospel of Matthew* (Grand Rapids, MI: Baker Books, 2001), 30.

6. What do you admire about these Magi? What can we learn from them?

Notice the magi weren't coming to get something from Jesus. After all, He was only a baby, a toddler there in Bethlehem. Nor were they coming because of what He had done for them; for at that point, He had done nothing. They came to worship Him solely because of who He was.

Do you ever come to church saying, "Lord, I'm going to worship You because I've got this business deal coming down next week, and I need Your help," or, "I'm feeling depressed, and I know if I worship, I'll get high emotionally and spiritually"?

There are, indeed, blessings to be found in worship, but they shouldn't be our motivation to worship. Why should we worship the Lord? Because He is the King of kings, the Creator of all things, the reason for life, the destiny of life. He is the smitten Rock, the Alpha and the Omega, the Lily of the Valley, the Fairest of Ten Thousand, the Bright and Morning Star. An understanding of who Jesus is should be motivation enough for us to worship Him. For truly, "Thou art worthy O Lord, to receive glory and honour and power" (Revelation 4:11). — Jon Courson, *Jon Courson's Application Commentary* (Nashville, TN: Thomas Nelson, 2003), 8–9.

7. How many Magi were there?

THERE ARE AT LEAST TWO historical inaccuracies in John Henry Hopkins's otherwise wonderful Christmas carol "We Three Kings." First is the number three. How many wise men were there? Were there three? Matthew doesn't provide such a detail. He just says "wise men from the east came to Jerusalem" (2:1). The plural subject of that sentence tells us there were more than one. Were there two? Were there twenty? We don't know. Well then, where do we get three? This tradition comes from the three gifts mentioned in verse 11, the logic being that if there were three gifts there must have been three men. But such logic is flawed, for if I told you I received a Rolex, a diamond-studded pinky ring, and a body-length mink coat for Christmas, these three gifts would not necessitate three givers, would they? If I told you that my wife gave me these three gifts this Christmas you might be surprised if you knew how frugal she is and that such gifts don't precisely fit my style. But you wouldn't be surprised if my wife gave me three gifts, would you? In fact, she did give me three gifts this year—a novel, a used theology book, and a stainless-steel coffee mug—all fitting gifts for my sanctified obsessions. — Douglas Sean O'Donnell, *Matthew:*

All Authority in Heaven and on Earth, ed. R. Kent Hughes, *Preaching the Word* (Wheaton, IL: Crossway, 2013), 59.

8. Why does the old Christmas carol call them "Kings"? (We three kings of orient are…) Is this right?

So the "three" in "We Three Kings" is not necessarily accurate. Neither is the description "kings." Again the gifts are to blame for this misunderstanding. Gold, frankincense, and myrrh were very expensive. Such gifts tell us that these men had abundant resources. They had money that allowed them to travel and to give Jesus what they gave him. But such wealth does not necessitate royalty.

I'm sorry to ruin what might be your favorite Christmas carol, but here in 2:1–12 there are not likely three kings. However, there are two! Matthew wants us to take note of two kings— King Herod and King Jesus. Look at verse 1, "Now after Jesus was born in Bethlehem of Judea in the days of Herod the king …" Look also at verses 3 and 9. Verse 3 begins, "When Herod the king …," and verse 9, "After listening to the king…." The first king is Herod.

The second king is obviously Jesus. Look at verse 2, where the wise men say of him, "Where is he who has been born king of the Jews?" Then, also in verse 2, they speak of "his star"— which most scholars believe is a reference to the oracle of Balaam, "a star shall come out of Jacob, and a scepter shall rise out of Israel" (Numbers 24:17). This "star" in the sky symbolizes to them this "star"—the coming of the ideal king, from the Jews, for the world. Look also at verse 4, where Herod inquires about "where the Christ was to be born." The Greek word for "Christ" means "anointed one" or "king." Also peek at the prophecy in verse 6 that speaks of "the rulers of Judah" and "a ruler" who is to come. So we have "his star," "the Christ," and "a ruler." These are all different words than "king," but are obviously on the same theme and about the same person.

This kingly theme as it relates to Jesus also fits the immediate context. It fits with the five fulfillments we examined in the last sermon, all of which have to do with Jesus being the King.

The prophets—Isaiah, Jeremiah, Micah, and Hosea—all speak of a king to come. It also fits the genealogy (1:1–17) and birth narrative (1:18–25), both of which emphasize Jesus' official relationship with King David. Finally, it fits what follows in chapters 3, 4, where King Jesus is introduced nearly three decades later by John the Baptist whose message is, "Repent, for the kingdom of heaven is at hand" (3:2), the same words Jesus will use in 4:17 as he begins his public ministry.

So, we two kings is what we have here—Herod and Jesus. As readers of this Gospel, our task now is to figure out (which won't be too difficult) which king is the true king, and thus the king to whom we should submit. — Douglas Sean O'Donnell, *Matthew: All Authority in Heaven and on Earth*, ed. R. Kent Hughes, *Preaching the Word* (Wheaton, IL: Crossway, 2013), 59–60.

9. What do these Magi teach us about Jesus?

Jesus is worthy of worship. Matthew illuminates Jesus' identity by emphasizing the worship of Jesus by the magi. Matthew, more than the other Gospel writers, portrays various characters worshiping Jesus in his story. In fact, Jesus is portrayed as an object of worship (with the verb proskyneō [rendered "knelt" at a number of points]) ten times, more than in the other three Gospels altogether (2:2, 8, 11; 8:2; 9:18; 14:33; 15:25; 20:20; 28:9, 17). These moments of worship include an emphasis at the beginning and the end of the Gospel: the magi worship Jesus at his birth (2:11), and his followers worship him upon his resurrection (28:9, 17). Not only does Matthew clarify his Christology through this emphasis on worship; he also provides a model for Christian practice. The proper response to Jesus the Messiah is worship. And accenting these portraits from Matthew's story can draw our own audiences into deeper worship and praise of Jesus the Messiah. — Jeannine K. Brown, Matthew, ed. Mark L. Strauss and John H. Walton, *Teach the Text Commentary Series* (Grand Rapids, MI: Baker Books, 2015), 26–27.

10. There is a lot of mystery with the Magi. One thing we do know—they were gentiles. What is the significance? What is the lesson/ application for us?

Keep in mind that these men were Gentiles. From the very beginning, Jesus came to be "the Saviour of the world" (John 4:42). These men were also wealthy, and they were scholars—scientists in their own right. No scholarly person who follows the light God gives him can miss worshiping at the feet of Jesus. In Jesus Christ "are hid all the treasures of wisdom and knowledge" (Col. 2:3). In Him dwells "all the fullness of the Godhead bodily" (Col. 2:9). — Warren W. Wiersbe, *The Bible Exposition Commentary, vol. 1* (Wheaton, IL: Victor Books, 1996), 14.

11. Matthew seems to be making a contrast between King Herod and King Jesus. How are they different?

Matthew makes our decision rather easy, doesn't he? Do you want a madman or the Messiah? Do you want a man who would order the massacre of innocent children (v. 16) or a man who would open his arms to children and lay down his life for the less-than-innocent of the world? Do you want a ruler who rules by force, aggression, and cruelty or a ruler who rules by love, compassion, and the cross of his own sufferings? Do you want a man who slaughtered the last remnants of the dynasty that ruled before him, put to death half of the Sanhedrin, killed 300 court officers, executed his wife and mother-in-law and three sons, and as he lay dying arranged for all the notable men of Jerusalem to be assembled in the Hippodrome and killed as soon as his own death was announced, so the people might weep instead of rejoice on the day of his death? Do you want him for king? Or do you want the One who when reviled did not revile in return, who when he suffered did not threaten but rather bore our sins in his body on the tree (see 1 Peter 2:21–25)? Whom do you want? Do you want the Big Bad Wolf or the Good Shepherd—a "shepherd king" like David, one who would finally and perfectly, as verse 6b puts it, "shepherd my people Israel" (cf. 2 Samuel. 5:2; Ezekiel 34)? — Douglas Sean O'Donnell, *Matthew: All Authority in Heaven and on*

Earth, ed. R. Kent Hughes, *Preaching the Word* (Wheaton, IL: Crossway, 2013), 60–61.

12. Verses 4, 5. What do you admire about the chief priest and teachers of the law?

Then there were the Jewish chief priests and scribes. Their attitude is almost as amazing as that of the Magi. They knew their Scriptures and had no problem in answering Herod when he wanted to know where the child would be born. Back came the answer, pointing Herod to Micah 5:2. He would be born in Bethlehem, of course. But did they go to greet him? Did they lift a sandal? Not at all. They knew it all, but they did nothing. That is a characteristic danger for clergy and scholars in any age. Their apathy hardened into outright opposition to Jesus as his ministry developed, and ended with frenzied lust for his blood—an awesome warning that knowledge is no substitute for obedience. — Michael Green, *The Message of Matthew: The Kingdom of Heaven, The Bible Speaks Today* (Leicester, England; Downers Grove, IL: InterVarsity Press, 2001), 67–68.

13. What do you *not* admire about the chief priests and teachers of the law?

The magi were seeking the King; Herod was opposing the King; and the Jewish priests were ignoring the King. These priests knew the Scriptures and pointed others to the Saviour, but they would not go to worship Him themselves! They quoted Micah 5:2 but did not obey it. They were five miles from the very Son of God, yet they did not go to see Him! The Gentiles sought and found Him, but the Jews did not. — Warren W. Wiersbe, *The Bible Exposition Commentary, vol. 1* (Wheaton, IL: Victor Books, 1996), 14–15.

14. Another old hymn speaks of "Jesus the Nazarene." Locate Nazareth on a map. How is it that Jesus was called a Nazarene?

There were doubtless people in Matthew's day who asserted that Jesus of Nazareth was born in Nazareth—and what people thought of Nazareth is made very plain in John

1:46. So Matthew puts the record straight. Jesus was not a Nazareth lad but born in Bethlehem, just as the prophet had foretold. Interestingly enough, Matthew does not know that Joseph was a native of Nazareth, although Luke knows it. On returning from Egypt, Joseph 'went and lived in a town called Nazareth' (23). Despite the common subject matter covered by Luke and Matthew in the stories of Jesus' birth, they are totally independent of each other. That independence lends an added strength to their testimony. — Michael Green, *The Message of Matthew: The Kingdom of Heaven, The Bible Speaks Today* (Leicester, England; Downers Grove, IL: InterVarsity Press, 2001), 68.

15. What does the gift of gold tell you about the Magi's view of baby Jesus?

It is easy to see why gold was an appropriate gift for Jesus Christ. Gold is the metal of kings. When gold was presented to Jesus by the men of Persia, it was an acknowledgment of his right to rule.

In his commentary on Matthew, William Barclay notes that according to Seneca, the distinguished Roman orator and writer, it was the custom in Persia that no one could approach a king without a gift and that "gold, the king of metals," was the proper gift for "a king of men." This is obvious from the discoveries of archaeologists. When a tomb is opened and is found to be filled with gold, it is usually proof that the deceased was a great person, most likely royalty. I have seen some of these gold relics. In Greece, in the ruins of the ancient city of Mycenae, dating from the time of the Trojan War, there is a cemetery in which the kings of the town were buried, and in the archeological museum at Athens, one can see the elaborate "death mask of Agamemnon," done in pure gold, which was discovered there. It is one of the greatest treasures of the ancient world. Similarly, in Cairo, the state museum contains the incredibly beautiful and literally priceless coffins and other tomb objects of King Tutankhamen, discovered in the Valley of the Kings at Thebes in 1922 by Howard Carter.

Some theologians have pointed out that when the wise men brought gold to the infant Jesus, they were being used by God to provide the funds necessary for Joseph to take the young child and his mother to Egypt to escape Herod's attempt on Jesus' life. This is probably true, but it is not as important as the significance of the gift itself. Jesus was a king, as the wise men knew and acknowledged (v. 2). He was the King of Kings. The wise men confessed his kingship when they presented their gift of gold. — James Montgomery Boice, *The Gospel of Matthew* (Grand Rapids, MI: Baker Books, 2001), 31.

16. What is frankincense?

It is also easy to see why incense was a significant and symbolic gift. Incense was used in the temple worship. It was mixed with the oil used to anoint the priests of Israel, and it was blended into the meal offerings that were presented to the priests by the people to be offered as thanksgiving and praise gifts to God. Incense gave an offering its pleasant odor, and Paul was probably thinking of incense when he compared the gifts of the Philippians to such a sacrifice, calling them "a fragrant offering, an acceptable sacrifice, pleasing to God" (Phil. 4:18). In presenting incense, the wise men, either intentionally or unintentionally, pointed to Christ as our great High Priest, the one whose entire life was pleasing to his Father.

It is interesting to note that incense was never mixed with sin offerings, which were meat and wine offerings. Only the meal offerings, which were not for sin, contained incense. When we remember that, we think naturally of Jesus, to whom the incense was given. He was without sin. When his enemies came to him on one occasion, he challenged them with the question, "Can any of you prove me guilty of sin?" (John 8:46). They were speechless. Earlier he had said of his Father, "I always do what pleases him" (John 8:29). None of us can say that. Since only the Lord Jesus Christ was sinless, it is fitting that incense was offered to him.

"We see from the symbolism of these gifts," wrote Donald Grey Barnhouse, that the eternal royalty and holiness of Christ were announced from his earliest years. He had come forth from heaven to perform the work of redemption, and he was prepared in every way to do the Father's will so that he might fulfill every demand and obligation of the law. Thus only would he become eligible to die on the cross; and by that cross alone redeem the world. That life could show that he was the fit candidate for the cross, and we cling with surety to the work that was accomplished there at Calvary, since we know that our sin-bearer was himself without sin.

James Montgomery Boice, *The Gospel of Matthew* (Grand Rapids, MI: Baker Books, 2001), 31–32.

17. Last gift: Myrrh. What is myrrh?

That observation leads naturally to the last and most significant of these gifts. Just as gold spoke of Christ's kingship and incense spoke of the perfection of his life, myrrh spoke of his death.

Myrrh was used in embalming. Because the trappings of death (although different) were as important then as today, myrrh was an important item of commerce in the ancient world. For instance, for Jesus' burial Nicodemus used one hundred pounds of myrrh and aloes to prepare the body. If one hundred pounds of that combination were used for just one body, a tremendous amount of myrrh must have been constantly bought and sold for funeral arrangements. Moreover, in Revelation 2 we read of a city of Asia Minor called Smyrna. The name is actually the Greek word for myrrh. The city was called Smyrna because its chief industry was the manufacture of myrrh.

By any human measure it would be odd, if not offensive, to present a spice used for embalming at the birth of a child. But it was not offensive in this case, nor was it odd. It was a gift of faith. Of course, we do not know exactly what the wise men may have surmised about Christ's future ministry or have intended by this gift, but we know from the Old Testament that Jesus' ministry was pictured again and again as one involving suffering. Psalm 22 describes Jesus' death by crucifixion; it was a verse from this psalm that Jesus quoted when he cried out from the cross, "My God, my God, why have you forsaken me?" (Ps. 22:1; see Matt. 27:46). Isaiah 53:4–5 says, "Surely he took up our infirmities and carried our sorrows, yet we considered him stricken by God, smitten by him, and afflicted. But he was pierced for our transgressions, he was crushed for our iniquities; the punishment that brought us peace was upon him, and by his wounds we are healed." Jesus came to suffer for our sin, and his suffering was symbolized by the Magi's gift of myrrh.

There was another use of myrrh in the ancient world that is important here; it was a use the Lord Jesus Christ refused. When he was about to be crucified and the soldiers offered him "wine mixed with myrrh," Jesus refused the offer (Mark 15:23). Myrrh was a crude anesthetic sometimes used to deaden pain, and Jesus wished to endure the full extent of suffering in his death for us. He was willing to bear all that the suffering and death entailed.

William Barclay says rightly, "Gold for a king, frankincense for a priest, myrrh for one that was to die—these were the gifts of the wise men, and, even at the cradle of Christ, they foretold that he was to be the true King, the perfect High Priest, and in the end the supreme Savior of men." — James Montgomery Boice, *The Gospel of Matthew* (Grand Rapids, MI: Baker Books, 2001), 32–33.

18. Summary. What do we learn about following God from the example of these wise men?

But enough about the wise men's gifts. Let's think about the Magi themselves. It is true that we do not know very much about these men, as I acknowledged earlier. We do not even know if they can properly be called wise men, since the word Matthew actually uses is magoi, rightly rendered "Magi" by the New International Version. Magoi actually means "great (or powerful) ones," and it indicates high position or influence. True enough! Nevertheless, these men were truly wise, and we would be wise to remember them and learn from them.

How were these men wise?

1. They were wise enough to seek Jesus. God had informed them of the birth of the new Jewish king, though we do not know exactly how. Realizing they were far from him, they did the wise thing. They prepared a traveling caravan and made their way to the capital city of the Jews. Moreover, when they got there and discovered that his birth was not a common topic of conversation, they asked people where he was. I notice that the story does not say the wise men asked their question of Herod first. In fact, they do not meet him until halfway through the story. They must have been asking everyone about Jesus and only came to Herod when their quest reached the monarch's ears.

Are you wise enough to seek Jesus? His birth has been announced well and widely. There is no mystery about it. Have you found him? If you have not yet found him, are you still seeking? A common contemporary saying asserts, "Wise men still seek him."

2. They were wise enough to seek information. There is another way in which the wise men were truly wise. They were wise enough to learn from others, even though there was little information to be had either from the people or their leaders. They were Magi, and in their own country, they were the ones from whom others sought information. They were the intellectuals of their culture. Some in their position would have been hindered by pride, but not these wise men. In this story they seek information, standing meekly as genuine disciples when the chief priests and teachers of the law opened the Scriptures and read to them from Micah 5:2: "But you, Bethlehem Ephrathah, though you are small among the clans of Judah, out of you will come for me one who will be ruler over Israel" (see Matt. 2:6).

What they learned when the Scriptures were opened to them was important. They learned that Christ was to be born in Bethlehem, a nearby town, and because they were wise, they must have understood that this was as significant for what it did not say as for what it did. We must suppose that the Magi were expecting to find the Lord Jesus Christ in Jerusalem, for that was the capital city and Jesus was the Jews' king. They probably expected to find Jesus in Herod's palace. But he was not there. In fact, the reigning king did not even know about his birth.

Not in the palace? Well, then, perhaps in the temple. Perhaps the new spiritual leader would be there. But Jesus was not to be found in the temple either. He had not emerged from the company of the priests or scribes. On the contrary, his birthplace was the little town of Bethlehem to the south of Jerusalem, an apparently insignificant spot, where the Scriptures had long ago indicated he would be born.

The wise men must have noticed that these teachers of the law were unspiritual and unworthy men, for they had so little interest in the birth of Israel's Messiah that they did not even accompany the Magi to Bethlehem to investigate his arrival for themselves. That did not bother the wise men. God was calling them to Christ, and his call would in time surely lead them to him. Their quest was so serious, their questions so earnest, that they were able to learn even from those who did not know where he was as well as from those, like the chief priests and teachers of the law, who knew but did not care. Above all, they were able to learn where Jesus was from the Bible.

Are you wise enough to find Jesus in the Bible? The wise men had to travel a long distance to find him, but no one has to travel a long distance today. The Bible says, "Do not say in your heart, 'Who will ascend into heaven?' (that is, to bring Christ down) or 'Who will descend into the deep?' (that is, to bring Christ up from the dead). But what does it say? 'The word is near you; it is in your mouth and in your heart,' that is, the word of faith we are proclaiming" (Rom. 10:6–8). Jesus is present in the gospel, and whoever calls on him will be saved.

3. They were wise enough to worship him when they found him. This point is very important, because some people seek even though they do not want to find the truth and embrace it. Paul spoke of these people when he warned Timothy of those who are "always learning but never able

to acknowledge the truth" (2 Tim. 3:7). Some people love unbelief, and they use their accumulating knowledge as justification for it. The wise men were not like this. They wanted to know about Jesus, but they were not interested in this knowledge for its own sake. They knew when they found him that they would worship him and give him their gifts. — James Montgomery Boice, *The Gospel of Matthew* (Grand Rapids, MI: Baker Books, 2001), 33–34.

19. **What do you want to recall from today's conversation?**

20. **How can we support one another in prayer this week?**

Lesson #4, Matthew 4.1 - 10
Good Questions Have Groups Talking
www.joshhunt.com

Matthew 4.1 - 10

OPEN

Let me ask each of you to share your name, what is the most wilderness-ish wilderness you have been to?

DIG

1. **Matthew 4.1 – 10. Overview. In this passage we find Jesus dealing with temptation. What do we learn about dealing with temptation from Jesus' example?**

   SPIRITUAL WARFARE. The Bible is an important tool to help us in this area.

   Jesus focused on the Scriptures when he was tempted by the Devil (Matt. 4:1–11). Also, the Word is the only offensive weapon in the listing of the armor of God, "so that you can take your stand against the devil's schemes" (Eph. 6:11–17). Satan has more power when there is a lack of truth and light. The Bible sheds truth and light in our lives and hearts so that he has less purchase on us. I have experienced situations in which I could tell that there were dark forces at work; when I quoted Scriptures, the effect was a lessening or ending of the attack. — Henry Cloud and John Townsend, *How People Grow: What the Bible Reveals about Personal Growth* (Grand Rapids, MI: Zondervan, 2009).

2. Three times Jesus said, "It is written." What is the application for us?

"It is written!" is a statement that carries great authority for the believer. Our Lord used the Word of God to defeat Satan, and so may we (Matt. 4:1–11; see Eph. 6:17). But the Word of God is not only a sword for battle; it is also a light to guide us in this dark world (Ps. 119:105; 2 Peter 1:19), food that strengthens us (Matt. 4:4; 1 Peter 2:2), and water that washes us (Eph. 5:25–27).

The Word of God has a sanctifying ministry in the lives of dedicated believers (John 17:17). Those who delight in God's Word, meditate on it, and seek to obey it will experience God's direction and blessing in their lives (Ps. 1:1–3). The Word reveals God's mind, so we should learn it; God's heart, so we should love it; God's will, so we should live it. Our whole being—mind, will, and heart—should be controlled by the Word of God. — Warren W. Wiersbe, *The Bible Exposition Commentary, vol. 2* (Wheaton, IL: Victor Books, 1996), 397.

3. Verse 1. Why do you think God led Jesus to be into the wilderness to be tempted?

Why did Jesus grow weary in Samaria (John 4:6), disturbed in Nazareth (Mark 6:6), and angry in the Temple (John 2:15)? Why was he sleepy in the boat on the Sea of Galilee (Mark 4:38), sad at the tomb of Lazarus (John 11:35), and hungry in the wilderness (Matt. 4:2)?

Why? Why did he endure all these feelings? Because he knew you would feel them too.

He knew you would be weary, disturbed, and angry. He knew you'd be sleepy, grief-stricken, and hungry. He knew you'd face pain. If not the pain of the body, the pain of the soul . . . pain too sharp for any drug. He knew you'd face thirst. If not a thirst for water, at least a thirst for truth, and the truth we glean from the image of a thirsty Christ is—he understands.

And because he understands, we can come to him. — *He Chose the Nails* / Max Lucado, *Grace for the Moment®*

*Volume Ii: More Inspirational Thoughts for Each Day of the Year (*Nashville: Thomas Nelson, 2006).

4. **One repeated phrase in this story is from the lips of Jesus: "It is written." Another is from the mouth of Satan. Why do you think he says, "IF you are the Son of God…"?**

Imagine that we overhear two businessmen in conversation. The first says, "This minor recession is not altogether negative. It gives us a breather, some time to evaluate the business and streamline our organization. The problem is the uncertainty. When will it end? Will business get worse before it turns around again?"

The second agrees, "So true. If I knew it would last another year, I would know how to cut back. I hate to think about layoffs. I can't afford to lose good people—especially if business heats up soon. I would rather know we had eight more soft months than live with this uncertainty. If only we knew…."

Next we see a woman walking briskly, consternation in her eye. She is thinking: "I looked Jennifer right in the eye and called out her name, but she hardly glanced at me. Is she mad at me or preoccupied? Is she upset about what I said last week? I'd rather know she is mad than wonder if something is wrong. If only I knew…."

Of course, we cannot know when business will turn around, nor do we know why an acquaintance turns away. Yet we want to know and want to know now. The desire to know is typically good, but it can become a sinful longing, a temptation to be all-knowing, like God. In fact, there may be no temptation more basic than the desire to have the knowledge—along with the other powers—of God.

In the garden, the serpent enticed Eve to eat from the tree of knowledge. If she did, he promised, "you will be like God, knowing good and evil" (Gen. 3:5). As we come to Jesus' temptations, we see that they parallel those of Adam and Eve in several ways. When Satan exhorts Jesus to jump from the temple, it is also a temptation touching knowledge. If Jesus jumps, then floats to the ground, he will know that the Father will care for him. — Daniel M. Doriani, Matthew & 2, ed. Richard D. Phillips, Philip Graham Ryken, and Daniel M. Doriani, vol. 1, *Reformed Expository Commentary* (Phillipsburg, NJ: P&R Publishing, 2008), 70–71.

5. **What would be some examples of temptations we regularly face? Let's make a long list.**

We usually think of temptation in flaming red colors. Flaming red temptation is seeing a wad of $100 bills drop from someone's pocket and trying to decide what to do next. Flaming temptation is going to a hotel room and finding that a quasi-pornographic movie is available for free. It is a beer offered to an alcoholic. It is a boss telling his staff he will not be looking closely at expense accounts. We do encounter flaming red temptations at times, but the Bible and experience both suggest that most temptations are gray. — Daniel M. Doriani, Matthew & 2, ed. Richard D. Phillips, Philip Graham Ryken, and Daniel M. Doriani, vol. 1, *Reformed Expository Commentary* (Phillipsburg, NJ: P&R Publishing, 2008), 71.

6. **Have you ever wondered how godly men—I am thinking now of preachers—sometimes go south? How does this happen? How does temptation begin?**

It starts with a flicker of thought, a tiny little idea that darts across the mind while you're doing something else. It seems harmless, just one of the millions of things that the human brain comes up with. But then it returns, a minute or an hour later. You feel it now as something familiar, and perhaps enticing. If I claim travel expenses for that trip, even though I had a ride from a friend ... if I had a chance to say that really cutting remark to the man who's always been mean to me ... if I played my cards right, I might persuade my friend's spouse to spend an evening with me, and then maybe ...

Always, to begin with, it seems quite reasonable, only just a bit off limits. But if we play with the idea, or allow it to play with us, then a new course is set, heading for disaster at one level or another. — Tom Wright, *Lent for Everyone: Matthew Year A* (London: SPCK, 2011), 9–10.

7. What are some temptations you personally face?

So there I was, standing in a hotel lobby with a strange woman, a throbbing heartbeat, and a guilty conscience. In most ways it wasn't nearly as bad as it looks typed out on this page. But in lots of ways it was even worse. I didn't really do anything wrong—and certainly didn't set out to do anything wrong. But that was just the problem. Before I knew it, I was scared at how mindless I was about the whole scenario.

I'd gotten here kind of accidentally. My family and I were driving—through the state of Tennessee, I think—when one of those sudden rainstorms had emerged, the kind that brings the slick grime right up to the surface of the road and mucks up the windshield with smearing drops the wipers can't seem to keep up with. Even though we hadn't gotten nearly as far as I'd hoped, the rain just wasn't letting up. I pulled the minivan off the highway and left my family in the vehicle while I ran in to check for a vacancy in a chain hotel whose sign we'd seen through the storm.

I waited in line at the front desk. I was exhausted and irritated, mostly because of the rain and the almost Hindu-like mantra coming from the backseat—"Dad, he's hitting me"—repeated over and over and over again. My thoughts were clicking around as I waited to check us in, moving from sermon ideas to budget numbers to parenting strategies.

The clerk, a young woman, gave an artificial pout and then a wink and a half smile, indicating she could tell it'd been a trying day. "Well, hey there," she said, and as soon as she said it I noticed she reminded me of a friend I'd known back in college. She had dimples in her cheeks, I think, and she tossed her hair back, holding it there in her hand for a minute as she checked on whether two adjoining rooms, one for my wife and me and one for the kids, would be available that night.

When she called me by my first name, I felt a little jump in my stomach—like the feeling you get in the split second when the roller coaster creaks to the top of the pinnacle, just before you can see the drop in front of you. I started to ask, "How do you know my name?" before I realized she was reading my credit card.

As this woman waited for the credit card machine to rattle out my receipt and punch out my automated key, we talked about the rain outside and about how traffic was bad because of the ball game at the high school stadium down the road. She laughed at my little quips. She teased me about my soaking wet hair from running through the stormy weather. I felt like I was in college again, or maybe even in high school. I didn't have to judge between disputes over who had whose toys or explain how predestination and free will work together in the Bible. I didn't have to pay a mortgage or tell a faculty member he couldn't have a raise. And I liked it.

Just then I heard a word I never thought would terrify me, but it did, just that once. I heard "Daddy." And then I heard it again. "Daddy!" my three-year-old son Samuel cried out as he rode through the lobby in the luggage cart being pushed by his two older brothers. "Look at me!"

I did look at him and wiped a bead of sweat from my forehead as I realized I had completely forgotten that my family was waiting outside for me in the van. As I signed the credit card form, I noticed that my voice and body language toward the clerk had suddenly become a good bit more businesslike. — Russell D. Moore, *Tempted and Tried: Temptation and the Triumph of Christ* (Wheaton, IL: Crossway, 2011).

8. **How do you picture this wilderness? If you have a smart phone, you might do a search for a picture. (You might show this video: https://youtu.be/ ixfYkAHjAgM)**

Author Barbara Brown Taylor recounts going to a seminar where a presenter talked about taking student groups out into the wilderness to experience in hiking and rafting "the untamed holiness of the wild." Brown writes that a participant raised his hand and asked whether "there are predators in those places who are above you on the food chain." The wilderness guide said that there weren't, of course, because he wouldn't take his students to a place where they would be so jeopardized. "I wouldn't either," the audience member replied, "but don't lull them into thinking that they have experienced true wilderness. It's only wilderness if there's something out there that can eat you." There's some wisdom there. For Jesus, there was something dark and ancient and predatory out there in the desert. — Russell D. Moore, *Tempted and Tried: Temptation and the Triumph of Christ* (Wheaton, IL: Crossway, 2011).

9. **Verse 2. Is it is really possible to go forty days without food? Can you think of other examples of people who fasted for a long time?**

Fasting for forty days was not unknown to those who studied the Scriptures and to the people of Israel familiar with their history. Exodus 34:28 says when Moses was given the Law on Mount Horeb, he neither ate nor drank for forty days. In 1 Kings 19, we read Elijah also fasted for forty days after the Lord sent an angel who gave him a certain kind of food that was able to sustain him for that period of time. Moses and Elijah both fasted forty days. Jesus fasted forty days, and later in Matthew's account, we will see how we are to act when we fast as well.

We live in a society addicted not only to alcohol and lust, but to all sorts of things. I suggest to you the reason could be because, as a society, we have ignored the simple principle of fasting, of saying no to the appetites of our bodies on a regular basis. If you feel an addictive pull in some area of your life, try saying no to your stomach's demands for a meal for a day or a week. When you deny the physical to concentrate on the spiritual, a dynamic occurs that I believe will very definitely help you overcome evil. — Jon Courson, *Jon Courson's Application Commentary* (Nashville, TN: Thomas Nelson, 2003), 20–21. Verse 3. The first temptation begins, "If you are the son of God…" Why do you suppose Satan started here? What is this temptation about? What is the lesson for us?

Who Are You?

The first step in the cycle of temptation is the question of your identity. James told the poor and the beaten down to "boast in his exaltation" and told the prosperous and the up-and-coming to glory "in his humiliation" (James 1:9–10). Why? James understood that temptation begins with an illusion about the self—a skewed vision of who you are. The satanic powers don't care if your illusion is one of personal grandiosity or of self-loathing, as long as you see your current circumstance, rather than the gospel, as the eternal statement of who you are. If the poor sees his poverty as making it impossible for him to have dignity, he is fallen. If the rich sees his wealth as a denial that "like a flower of the grass he will pass away," even "in the midst of his pursuits" (James 1:10–11), then he is undone.

Temptation has always started here, from the very beginning of the cosmic story. When the Bible reveals the ancestral fall of the human race, it opens with a question of identity. The woman in the Genesis narrative was approached by a mysterious serpent, a "beast of the field" that was "more crafty" than any of the others (Gen. 3:1). And that's just the point. The woman, Eve, and her husband were created in the image of God (Gen. 1:26–27). They were living signs of God's dominion over everything except God and one another. This dominion was exhaustive, right down to "every creeping thing that creeps on the earth" (Gen. 1:26).

But here she was being interrogated by a "beast of the field" that questioned God's commands and prerogatives. Without even a word, the serpent led the woman to act as though he had dominion over her instead of the other way around. He persuaded her to see herself as an animal instead of as what she had been told she was—the image-bearing queen of the universe, a principality and power over the beasts.

At the same time the serpent was treating his queen as a fellow animal, he also subtly led her to see herself as more than an empress—as a goddess. He auditioned her for her role as deity by leading her to act like a god, distinguishing autonomously between good and evil, deciding when she and her fellow were ready for maturity, evaluating the claims of God himself. The snake prompted her to eat the fruit of the tree God had forbidden to her. The tree somehow carried within it the power to awaken the conscience to "the knowledge of good and evil" (Gen. 2:17). The serpent walked the woman along to where she could see herself as if she were the ultimate cosmic judge, free from the scrutiny of her Creator's holiness. At the very beginning of the human story was a question: Who are you? — Russell D. Moore, *Tempted and Tried: Temptation and the Triumph of Christ* (Wheaton, IL: Crossway, 2011).

10. Why would it have been wrong for Jesus to eat bread? What is wrong with eating bread?

The three temptations here, like most if not all temptations, are good things that are being distorted. Bread is good. Jesus will later create a huge amount of it from a few loaves, to feed hungry people. But should he do that just for himself—and just to satisfy himself that he really is the 'Son of God', as the heavenly voice at his baptism had said? No: Jesus will satisfy himself with what God has said, rather than with any attempt to prove it. — Tom Wright, *Lent for Everyone: Matthew Year A* (London: SPCK, 2011), 10.

11. Jesus dealt with temptation by quoting scripture. How did He learn this scripture? What can we learn from His example?

You know what helps me when I sense I'm in the presence of the enemy? Nothing works better for me in resisting the Devil than the actual quoting of Scripture. I usually quote God's Word in such situations. One of the most important reasons for maintaining the discipline of Scripture memory is to have it ready on our lips when the enemy comes near and attacks. And you'll know it when he does. I don't know how to describe it, but the longer you walk with God, the more you will be able to sense the enemy's presence.

And when you do, you need those verses of victory ready to come to the rescue. The Word of God is marvelously strong. It is alive and active and "sharper than a two-edged sword." And its truths can slice their way into the invisible, insidious ranks of the demonic hosts.

Although our own strength is insufficient to fend him off, when we draw on the limitless resources of faith, we can stand against him nose-to-nose, much like I did with that intruder at Cancun. And such faith is nurtured and strengthened by a steady intake of the Scriptures.

Furthermore, the strength that comes from faith is supplemented by the knowledge of that company of saints stretching down through history, as well as present-day believers joining hands in prayer across the globe. There is something wonderfully comforting about knowing that we are not alone in the battle against the adversary. — Charles R. Swindoll, *Laugh Again & Hope Again* (Nashville: Thomas Nelson, 2009).

12. Do you think it is important that Christians memorize Scripture?

Two brothers were walking on their father's extensive, wooded acreage when they came upon a young tree heavy with fruit. Both enjoyed as much of the delicious fruit as they wanted. When they started back, one man gathered all the remaining fruit and took it home with him. His brother, however, took the tree itself and planted it on his own property. The tree flourished and regularly produced a bountiful crop so that the second brother often had fruit when the first had none.

The Bible is like the fruit-bearing tree in this story. Merely hearing the Word of God is to be like the first brother. You may gather much fruit from the encounter and even bring home enough to feed on for a few days, but in the long run it doesn't compare with having your own tree. Through the Disciplines of reading and studying, we make the tree our own and enjoy its fruit. Among the Spiritual Disciplines we also find the tools of memorization, meditation, and application, which bountifully increase our harvest of fruit from the tree. — Donald S. Whitney, *Spiritual Disciplines for the Christian Life* (Colorado Springs, CO: NavPress, 1991), 41.

13. What good things come to those who memorize scripture?

In his book, How To Study the Bible for Yourself, Tim LaHaye lists seven things that Scripture memory can do for you:

1.　It will give you victory over sin.

2.　It helps you overcome worry.

3.　It will give you a confidence in sharing your faith.

4.　It speeds up the transforming process.

5.　It assists you in discovering God's will for your life.

6.　It helps in your other Bible studies.

7.　It outfits you for unlimited service to God.

Robert J. Morgan, *Nelson's Complete Book of Stories, Illustrations, and Quotes*, electronic ed. (Nashville: Thomas Nelson Publishers, 2000), 61.

14. Suppose a friend said, "I can't memorize scripture; I just can't memorize." How would you respond?

Most people think they have a bad memory, but it's not true. As we've already discovered, most of the time memorizing is mainly a problem of motivation. If you know your birthday, phone number, and address, and can remember the names of your friends, then you can memorize Scripture. The question becomes whether you are willing to discipline yourself to do it.

When Dawson Trotman, founder of the Christian organization called The Navigators, was converted to faith in Christ in 1926, he began memorizing one Bible verse every day. He was driving a truck for a lumber yard in Los Angeles at the time. While driving around town he would work on his verse for that day. During the first three years of his Christian life he memorized his first thousand verses. If he could memorize over three hundred verses a year while driving, surely we can find ways to memorize a few. — Donald S. Whitney, *Spiritual Disciplines for the Christian Life* (Colorado Springs, CO: NavPress, 1991), 44–45.

15. Is anyone familiar with a good app to help with Scripture memory?

I just found an app I am really excited about. https://scripturetyper.com

16. Psalm 119.9, 11. What benefit do these verse promise to those who memorize Scripture?

How do I get rid of these youthful sins, these tendencies of my flesh? The psalmist says it is done by paying close attention to the Word. Let the Word of God, which is likened to water (Ephesians 5:26), flood your soul and cleanse you constantly.

I challenge you to consider memorizing at least a couple of verses a week. It's sad to me that we are living in a time when people no longer make this a part of their spiritual practice because it's a wonderful thing to do. Write verses that particularly speak to you on 3x5-inch cards, pack them around with you—and before you know it, you'll have a heart full of the Word and a life that reflects it. — Jon Courson, *Jon Courson's Application Commentary: Volume Two: Psalms-Malachi* (Nashville, TN: Thomas Nelson, 2006), 148.

17. Will Scripture memory alone make you a better Christian? What else is needed?

The Sadducees in Jesus' day probably knew the Scriptures (our Old Testament) better than nearly all Christians today.

But Jesus told them: " 'You are in error because you do not know the Scriptures or the power of God' " Matthew 22:29. They knew the words of the Scripture, but in their hearts they did not know its meaning or its power.

As you memorize Scripture make sure that you don't think this will by itself make you a better Christian. Unless the verses sink into your soul, there will be little change in your life. — Mark Water, *Scripture Memory Made Easy, The Made Easy Series* (Alresford, Hampshire: John Hunt Publishers Ltd, 1999), 9.

18. What are some keys to successful scripture memory?

No principle of Scripture memory is more important than the principle of review. Without adequate review you will eventually lose most of what you memorize. But once you really learn a verse, you can mentally review it in a fraction of the time it would take to speak it. And when you know a verse this well, you don't have to review but once a week, once a month, or even once every six months to keep a sharp edge on it. It's not unusual, however, to reach a point where you spend 80 percent of your Scripture memory time in review. Don't begrudge devoting so much time to polishing your swords. Rejoice instead at having so many!

A great time to review your better-known verses is while going to sleep. Since you don't need a written copy of the verses before you, you can repeat them and meditate on them while dozing off or even when you have trouble sleeping. And if you can't stay awake, it's fine, since you're supposed to be sleeping anyway. If you can't go to sleep, you're putting the most profitable and peaceful information possible into your mind, as well as making good use of the time.

As we finish this section on the Discipline of Scripture memory, remember that memorizing verses is not an end in itself. The goal is not to see how many verses we can memorize, the goal is Godliness. The goal is to memorize the Word of God so that it can transform our minds and our lives.

Dallas Willard said in this regard, "As a pastor, teacher, and counselor I have repeatedly seen the transformation of inner and outer life that comes simply from memorization and meditation upon Scripture. Personally, I would never undertake to pastor a church or guide a program of Christian education that did not involve a continuous program of memorization of the choicest passages of Scripture for people of all ages." — Donald S. Whitney, *Spiritual Disciplines for the Christian Life* (Colorado Springs, CO: NavPress, 1991), 46–47.

19. Verse 11. The Devil left Him. What is the good news for us?

But I have good news for you. Better still, Scripture has good news for you. When you resist through the power and in the name of the Lord Jesus Christ, the Devil will ultimately retreat. He will back down. He won't stay away; he'll back away. He will retreat as you resist him, firm in your faith.

Remember Ephesians 6:10–11: "Be strong in the Lord, and in the strength of His might. Put on the full armor of God, that you may be able to stand firm against the schemes of the devil."

This is where the Christian has the jump on every unbeliever who tries to do battle against the enemy. Those without the Lord Jesus have no power to combat or withstand those supernatural forces. No chance! They are facing the enemy without weapons to defend themselves. But when the Christian is fully armed with the armor God provides, he or she is invincible. Isn't that a great word? Invincible! That gives us hope beyond the battle.

It's a mockery to say to those who are not Christians, "Just stand strong against the enemy." They can't. They have no equipment. They have no weapons. A person must have the Lord Jesus reigning within to be able to stand strong in His might. — Charles R. Swindoll, *Laugh Again & Hope Again* (Nashville: Thomas Nelson, 2009).

20. Verse 11. Why do you think Jesus needed the angels to attend to Him? What was He feeling?

In spite of faith and in spite of friends, however, the battle is exhausting. I don't know of anything that leaves you more wrung out, more weary. Nothing is more demanding, nothing more emotionally draining, nothing more personally painful than encountering and resisting our archenemy.

The devil always has a strategy, and he is an excellent strategist. He's been at it since he deceived Eve in the Garden. He knows our every weakness. He knows our hardest times in life. He knows our besetting sins. He knows the areas where we tend to give in the quickest. He also knows the moment to attack. He is a master of timing . . . and he knows the ideal place. — Charles R. Swindoll, *Laugh Again & Hope Again* (Nashville: Thomas Nelson, 2009).

21. Summary. What difference does the temptation of Christ 2,000 years ago make to our lives today?

The Son of God became the Son of man, Immanuel—"God with us" (Matt. 1:23)—for very crucial reasons. Until Christ became the Son of man, He could not die in our place for our sins. God does not die; flesh and blood die. Christ became flesh and blood and maintained His perfect divinity so that He could pay the penalty of sin, which is death:

God demonstrates His own love toward us, in that while we were still sinners, Christ died for us. (Rom. 5:8)

This is My blood of the covenant, which is poured out for many for forgiveness of sins. (Matt. 26:28 NASB)

Until Christ became the Son of man, He could not represent us as our sympathetic and faithful High Priest. Christ understands how we feel in our frail humanity. He was weary (John 4:6), hungry (Matt. 4:2), rejected (Luke 4:28–30), and abused (Mark 15:16–20).

His earthly ministry means that Christ can identify with your hurts, pains, and heartaches. He is touched by them:

When the Lord saw her, He felt compassion for her, and said to her, "Do not weep." (Luke 7:13 NASB) — *Jesus wept.* (John 11:35) / Charles F. Stanley, *Enter His Gates: A Daily Devotional* (Nashville: Thomas Nelson Publishers, 1998).

22. How can we support one another in prayer this week?

Lesson #5, Matthew 5.1 - 16

Good Questions Have Groups Talking

www.joshhunt.com

Matthew 5.1 - 16

OPEN

Let's each share your name and complete this sentence:
"One thing that makes me happy is…"

DIG

1. **"Blessed" is clearly the theme of this passage. What does it mean to be blessed?**

   Yes, every human being ever born yearns for peace, purpose, and God Himself. But can we know these? Can our search be ended? Will our quest for true happiness ever be satisfied? The Bible declares a resounding "Yes!" And in these eight Beatitudes Jesus points the way. In each one of the Beatitudes—which someone has called the "beautiful attitudes"—Jesus used the word blessed. This word blessed is actually a very difficult word to translate into modern English, because in the original Greek language of the New Testament it has a far richer meaning than the everyday content of our English word. As we noted at the beginning of this chapter, the Amplified Version of the New Testament defines it as "happy, to be envied, and spiritually prosperous . . . with life-joy and satisfaction. . . ." But perhaps the word happy comes as close as any single English word to conveying the idea of "blessed" to us today, and that is the word we will use for the most part through this book. But let us never forget that the "blessedness" of which Jesus speaks is far, far deeper than any superficial happiness which comes and goes according to circumstances. That is why the word blessed guards well against its reduction and perversion.

Jesus' first words were: "Happy are ye." In those three words He was telling us that there is an answer to our search! We can know peace. We can know the truth about our lives. We can know God. And because of that, we can be blessed! — Billy Graham, *The Secret of Happiness* (Nashville: Thomas Nelson, 2002).

2. **Some translations have the word "happy" instead of "blessed." Is Jesus talking about how to be happy? To what degree is the Bible as a whole concerned with our happiness?**

Asher is consistently translated in the Greek Old Testament (the Septuagint) with the word makarios. Makarios, in turn, is used fifty times in the New Testament —more than half by Jesus. One scholar told me, "When you read makarios in the New Testament, think asher. That's how closely the words are related."[416]

One of the central and most definitive terms in the entire book of Psalms is the word asher. In fact, it's the first word of the entire book. In his highly acclaimed exegetical handbook on the Psalms, Hebrew and Old Testament professor Mark Futato demonstrates how Psalms 1 and 2 set forth the major themes of the entire book. He affirms that the two central themes of Psalms are "instruction for happiness" and "instruction for holiness."[417]

Since some see the English word happy as having a limited emotional connotation, Futato proposes that, with its implication of well-being, "truly happy" is a better rendering. [418]

Since asher occurs in all five sections within the Psalms (twenty-six times in all), Futato concludes, "The book of Psalms is an instruction manual for living a truly happy life."[419]

Here are examples of other scholars' comments to demonstrate the consensus about the meaning of asher:

- "Both [Psalm 119 and Psalm 1] begin with the word Blessed, a word that could be best translated as 'happy.'"[420]

- "The word 'blessed' means 'happy.'"[421]

- "Blessed —literally, 'oh, the happiness' —an exclamation of strong emotion."[422]

- "The Hebrew word . . . means that such a person is happy, or fortunate, deserving congratulations."[423]

- "[Asher] can be literally rendered 'happy.'"[424]

- "An emphatic Happy . . . describes the righteous person. The meaning is 'O the blessedness, the joy, the good fortune!'"[425]

I've come across dozens of similar statements from leading commentaries and Hebrew scholars who explain that asher means "happy." Many of these sources also comment that the English blessed means "happy." — Randy Alcorn, *Happiness* (Carol Stream, IL: Tyndale, 2015).

3. What does the English word "blessed" mean? What does the word mean outside of church?

Everyone knows it's good to be blessed, but what does that word actually mean?

Someone wrote me, "Your books have blessed me." I think they meant, "Your books have been of spiritual benefit." Though I hope it's also true, I doubt they meant, "Your books made me happy." Otherwise, they simply would have said that.

I googled "blessed," and the first hit was this definition: "Adjective: made holy; consecrated." Followed by "Noun: those who live with God in Heaven."

There are more than 2.5 million online references to the "blessed virgin Mary." Does anyone suppose this phrase means the "happy virgin Mary"? No. The reference is to her sanctity, not her gladness.

The third most popular hit for "blessed" was "Synonyms and antonyms for blessed."[413] Here are the listed synonyms: "adored, beatified, consecrated, divine, enthroned, exalted, glorified, hallowed, redeemed, resurrected, revered, rewarded, saved, among the angels, holy, inviolable, sacred, sacrosanct, spiritual, unprofane."

In the Merriam-Webster Unabridged Dictionary, the first synonym listed in the definition of blessed is "of, relating to, or being God."[414] Then the following synonyms are listed: "divine, godlike, godly, heavenly, sacred, supernatural." Under "related words," the dictionary adds, "eternal, everlasting, immortal; all-powerful, almighty, omnipotent, omniscient, supreme." The second definition of the word blessed is "set apart or worthy of veneration by association with God." The synonyms here include "consecrate, consecrated, hallowed, sacral, sacred, sacrosanct, sanctified."

Notice that every definition and synonym cited for blessed relates to holiness. Virtually nothing relates to happiness.

The Oxford English Dictionary's first definition of blessed is "consecrated, hallowed, holy; consecrated by a religious rite or ceremony." The second is "the object of adoring reverence, adorable, worthy to be blessed by men."[415] Only a third and remote definition involves happiness. Shorter modern dictionaries don't even list "happy" as a possible definition of blessed. Happiness is, for the most part, completely off the blessed radar. — Randy Alcorn, *Happiness* (Carol Stream, IL: Tyndale, 2015).

4. Are "blessed" and "happy" the same thing or something different?

I couldn't locate an official poll concerning what people today think blessed means, so I asked people on my Facebook page, "What comes to mind when you hear the word blessed?"

More than 1,100 responses followed, with 904 people offering specific meanings for blessed.

Some associated blessed with being "covered," "favored," or having peace and contentment. Five percent said that blessed meant "lucky" to them, while 21 percent thought blessed means "lucky" to unbelievers.

About 30 percent of responders mentioned "undeserved favor" from God, as most would define grace.

Here's a sampling of verbatim responses to what the term blessed brought to mind:

- Things going well.

- Someone who has it all and has had an easy life.

- Talented; privileged.

- Having my needs met.

- A showering of mercies from God.

- Being protected by God.

- To have something others want.

- Before I knew God, I thought blessed was creepy . . . like a cult term.

- Some kind of anointing.

- To be set apart/holy.

- Disguised bragging, as in, "Look at my new, expensive car. I'm so blessed."

- Being comfortable —a vaguely positive, churchy word.

Only 12 percent of those who answered the question made any mention whatsoever of happiness, gladness, or joy. In two cases where happiness was mentioned, respondents said they'd heard this connection from a pastor, but they were skeptical. One person said, "I think of blessed as being happy, but I know that isn't right."

One respondent said, "If my unbelieving friends hear me say 'blessed,' it doesn't have any concrete meaning to them; it's just part of a different worldview." Another said, "To unbelievers, it is Christianese. I doubt the current meaning attracts them to the gospel." — Randy Alcorn, *Happiness* (Carol Stream, IL: Tyndale, 2015).

5. Has the English word "blessed" changed its meaning since the KJV was released?

WHEN THE KJV TRANSLATORS RENDERED ASHER AND MAKARIOS "BLESSED," THEIR AUDIENCES KNEW IT MEANT "HAPPY."

John Wycliffe's first English translation of the Bible, hand printed and published in 1382, translated asher as "blessed" in Proverbs 28:14. The King James Version, published in 1611, usually translates asher as "blessed," but Proverbs 28:14 reads, "Happy is the man that feareth . . ."

Since happy was a synonym for blessed in those eras, it didn't make much difference which term was chosen. Today, however, it makes a great difference. When people read this verse as "Blessed is the one who fears the Lord always" or "Blessed is the one who always trembles before God" (NIV), they naturally understand blessed to mean something closer to "holy" than "happy."

Approximately 80 percent of the time, translators of the KJV followed the wording of Tyndale's translation.[427] In passage-to-passage text comparisons, the ESV and the NASB follow the KJV roughly 70 percent of the time.[428] Tyndale could have translated asher as "happy." He could have done the same with makarios in Matthew 5: "Happy are the poor in spirit" instead of "Blessed are the poor in spirit." Since the word blessed at that time conveyed the concept of happiness, his translation was accurate. But is it still accurate today?

THE EARLY TRANSLATORS INTENDED BLESSED TO CONVEY HAPPINESS.

The Letters of the Martyrs includes this passage written by Bishop Nicholas Ridley (1500–1555) shortly before he was burned at the stake in Oxford:

> For his truth's sake, then are ye happy and blessed, for the glory of the Spirit of God resteth upon you. If for rebuke's sake, suffered in Christ's name, a man is pronounced by the mouth of that holy apostle blessed and happy, how much more happy and blessed is he that hath the grace to suffer death also.[429]

Like other English clergy of his day, Ridley, a contemporary of William Tyndale, used blessed and happy as synonyms to reinforce each other's meanings.

At least 120 times in his writing, Puritan Thomas Brooks used the phrase "happiness and blessedness," just as we might describe a day as "bright and sunny." He spoke of "soul-happiness and blessedness"[430] and said, "So shall I know God according to my capacity . . . face to face; and this is the greatest height of blessedness and happiness."[431]

William Shakespeare (1564–1616) wrote of a man who discovered happiness in his misfortune. Notice how he paralleled happiness and blessedness: "His overthrow heap'd happiness upon him; For then, and not till then, he felt himself, And found the blessedness of being little."[432]

For several centuries thereafter, blessedness and happiness remained nearly interchangeable in common speech. Cambridge University professor and evangelical pastor Charles Simeon (1759–1836) said, "'Well done, good and faithful servant, enter thou into the joy of thy Lord;' if, further, you could behold it in the very bosom of its God, invested with a happiness which can never be interrupted, and a glory that shall never end; then you would say that its blessedness is truly wonderful"[433] (emphasis added).

I found this in the 1828 edition of Noah Webster's dictionary:

BLESS'ED, pp. Made happy or prosperous; extolled; pronounced happy. BLESS'ED, a. Happy; prosperous in worldly affairs; enjoying spiritual happiness and the favor of God; enjoying heavenly felicity.[434]

Likewise, Webster defined blessedly as "happily" and blessedness as "happiness." Two hundred years ago, people still understood blessed to mean "happy." That's a striking contrast to the results of my poll on what blessed means to people today.

BLESSED IS ONE OF MANY ENGLISH WORDS THAT HAVE CHANGED THEIR MEANINGS SINCE 1611.

It's common for word meanings to change over the centuries. For instance, the KJV says that the head of John the Baptist was put on a "charger" (Mark 6:25). Nearly every modern translation says "platter." In 1611 the word charger meant "platter" —so it was accurate.

Titus 2:14 speaks of Christ, "who gave himself for us, that he might redeem us from all iniquity, and purify unto himself a peculiar people" (KJV). Some of us Christ-followers may indeed be strange, but four hundred years ago, peculiar meant "singular" or "unique."

KJV scholars were usually correct to translate as they did in 1611. However, modern translators are also correct to depart from the King James when words no longer reflect the meaning of the Hebrew and Greek text to modern readers. Translations should convey the original meaning of the source language most closely expressed by words in the target language. That's why it doesn't make sense to continue to translate the Hebrew and Greek words that mean "happy" into the English word blessed.

Here's another illustration that shows the importance of this issue: Psalm 127:5 says, "Blessed [asher] is the man who fills his quiver with [children]!" (NASB). The NIV and the ESV also translate asher as "blessed." The KJV, the RSV, and YLT render it "happy."

Read the following translations and ask yourself whether happy conveys a significantly different understanding than blessed in this context. Remember, the "arrows" spoken of are children:

- Happy is the man who has many such arrows. (Psalm 127:5, GNT)

- The person who fills a quiver full with them is truly happy! (Psalm 127:5, CEB)

Readers who see "blessed" might think, Sure, God views children as a blessing and parents may too —when they're getting enough sleep! But in the meantime, having lots of children is nothing but sacrifice and stress!

The God-inspired text, however, connects child rearing with happiness. While this in no way suggests that having children is easy or is the only happiness, this text affirms that we should find great happiness in children.

"Blessed" may feel as comfortable as old slippers in such passages, especially for readers who are accustomed to the KJV. But surely the job of Bible translation is not to hang on to spiritual-sounding words when doing so cloaks the original meaning. — Randy Alcorn, *Happiness* (Carol Stream, IL: Tyndale, 2015).

6. I have heard preachers say that God doesn't care so much about your happiness as your holiness. Is that right?

Preaching on Psalm 1, which begins with the Hebrew word asher, Spurgeon said, "It is an old saying, and possibly a true one, that every man is seeking after happiness. If it is so, then every man should read this Psalm, for this directs us where happiness is to be found in its highest degree and purest form!"[426]

But if the scholars agree that asher means "happy," then why isn't it translated "happy"? That's an important question.

Some Bible versions use the formal equivalency method of translation, which is a literal, word-for-word approach. Others follow the functional equivalency method, which is a dynamic, thought-for-thought approach.

The most word-for-word translation of all, Young's Literal Translation, renders asher and makarios as "happy" the vast majority of the time. It translates asher as "blessed" only twice, one of which refers to God (see Isaiah 30:18). Similarly, it renders makarios "blessed" only twice, both of which refer to God (see 1 Timothy 1:11; 6:15).

The three translations that choose "happy" over "blessed" most frequently are the New Revised Standard Version, the Holman Christian Standard Bible, and Young's Literal Translation —all more literal, not dynamic, translations.

In maintaining the word blessed from centuries-old English translations, the New International Version, the English Standard Version, and the New American Standard Bible, as well as other translations, are more traditional but not more literal. — Randy Alcorn, *Happiness* (Carol Stream, IL: Tyndale, 2015).

7. **What do we learn about how to be happy from the beatitudes?**

Faith, family, and friends all contributed to happiness. According to Time, "Love, friendship, family . . . the belief that your life has purpose—these are the essentials of human fulfillment, and they can't be purchased with cash." — Greg Laurie, *Walking with Jesus: Daily Inspiration from the Gospel of John* (Grand Rapids, MI: Baker, 2007).

8. **What does it mean to be poor in spirit and how does it contribute to our happiness?**

In fact, the Bible doesn't anywhere commend poverty. Nor does it condemn wealth. Being poor in spirit has nothing to do with your bank account or 401(k). The word poor is from a verb meaning to shrink, cower, or cringe, as beggars often did in that day. This is speaking of a person who is destitute and completely dependent on others for help. Again, however, Jesus is not speaking in financial terms here. He is speaking of people who see themselves as they really are before God. They are lost, hopeless, and helpless. The truth is, apart from Jesus Christ and His provision of grace, everyone is spiritually destitute or poor in spirit, regardless of education, wealth, accomplishments, or even religious knowledge. To be poor in spirit means to acknowledge your spiritual bankruptcy and your total need of God.

Maybe you haven't been able to bring yourself to do this. Maybe you imagine that, after all, you have something to bring to the table.

No, you don't. You don't bring anything to the table. You are depraved, you are a sinner, and you are in desperate need of a Savior. It is His grace and His mercy being offered to you.

A person who is poor in spirit sees that. But it is difficult for some people to accept. In fact, some never do, and they never gain the kingdom of heaven. — Greg Laurie, *Worldview: Learning to Think and Live Biblically* (Dana Point, CA: Kerygma Publishing—Allen David Books, 2012).

9. How can those who mourn be happy?

To mourn for your sins is a natural outflow of poverty of spirit. The second beatitude should follow the first. But that's not always the case. Many deny their weakness. Many know they are wrong, yet pretend they are right. As a result, they never taste the exquisite sorrow of repentance.

Of all the paths to joy, this one has to be the strangest. True blessedness, Jesus says, begins with deep sadness.

"Blessed are those who know they are in trouble and have enough sense to admit it." — Max Lucado, *The Applause of Heaven* (Dallas, TX: Word Pub., 1996), 55.

10. What does it mean to be meek and how does it contribute to our happiness?

What, then, did Jesus mean? The dictionary says that the word meek means "mild, submissive, and compliant." William Barclay points out that the Greek word for "meek" was the word which was often used to describe an animal which had been tamed to obey the command of its master. It might be a strong animal like a horse or ox, able to do a great deal of work. It was not "weak"— but it was "meek," always obedient to the will of its owner. A tame horse contributes much more to life than a wild one. Energy out of control is dangerous; energy under control is powerful. — Billy Graham, *The Secret of Happiness* (Nashville: Thomas Nelson, 2002).

11. The fourth beatitude speaks of hungering and thirsting for righteousness. How is this different from the first three beatitudes?

Now comes a shift of emphasis. Whereas the first three Beatitudes are passive, this one has an active element to it. In speaking of those who are 'poor in spirit', 'mourn' and are 'meek', Jesus has been describing what these people are; now he turns to describe what certain people do. This is obvious from the text, nor is it difficult to see how the logical progression is maintained. Those who have a true sense of their sinfulness and a holy hatred for sin, and accept that they have no right to be favourably treated either by God or by other people, have also come to realize not only that they are spiritually destitute and helpless, but that they are utterly undeserving of either sympathy or help. It is to these people that Jesus says, 'Blessed are those who hunger and thirst for righteousness, for they will be filled.' — John Blanchard, *The Beatitudes for Today* (Leominster, UK: Day One Publications, 1996), 138.

12. Verse 6. Does following God make us satisfied or thirsty?

Lord, help me to pray as Tozer prayed:

> O God, I have tasted Thy goodness, and it has both satisfied me and made me thirsty for more. I am painfully conscious of my need of further grace. I am ashamed of my lack of desire. O God, the Triune God, I want to want Thee; I long to be filled with longing; I thirst to be made more thirsty still. Show me Thy glory, I pray Thee, so that I may know Thee indeed. Begin in mercy a new work of love within me. Say to my soul, "Rise up, my love, my fair one, and come away." Then give me grace to rise and follow Thee up from this misty lowland where I have wandered so long. In Jesus name. Amen.

Discipleship Journal, Issue 85 (January/February 1995) (NavPress, 1995).

13. What if I don't hunger and thirst for righteousness? What if righteousness is not all that important to me?

We talked about the fact that the phrase "poor in spirit" of verse three means recognizing that you are destitute of any righteous thing and are morally bankrupt. We cannot help ourselves. We are hopeless. We are sinful. And that is followed by, "they that mourn." That is the response to your broken spirit: mourning. Then there is meekness, and meekness says, "In comparison to God, I am nothing!" Meekness is humility. In our meekness before God, we realize that the only hope we ever have of knowing righteousness is to seek it at His hand. That brings us to the fourth Beatitude, and we hunger and thirst after what we know is not ours.

So the progression is simple. Martyn Lloyd–Jones wrote,

> This Beatitude follows logically from the previous one. See, it is a statement to which all the others lead. It is the logical conclusion to which they come. It is something for which we should all be profoundly thankful and grateful

to God. I do not know of a better test that anyone can apply to himself or herself in this whole matter of the Christian profession, than a verse like this. If this verse is to you one of the most blessed statements of the whole of Scripture, you can be quite sure you're a Christian. If it is not, you had better examine your foundations again.

John MacArthur, *The Beatitudes: The Only Way to Happiness* (Chicago: Moody Press, 1998).

14. Verse 7. Is this saying that being merciful to others is the way to earn God's mercy?

The sequel to mercy is obtaining mercy. What a beautiful thing. Do you see the cycle? God gives us mercy, we are merciful, and God gives us more mercy. Second Samuel 22:26 says the same thing, that it is the merciful who receive mercy. James 2:13 says it negatively, "For judgment will be merciless to one who has shown no mercy." It's there in Psalm 18 and Proverbs 14.

But now we must be warned of something, and this is critical: Some people think being merciful is how we get saved. This is the error of the Roman Catholic Church, that God is satisfied and gives mercy when we do merciful deeds. That view spawned monasteries and nunneries and everything related to them. But this is not the way to earn salvation. We do not get mercy for merit. Mercy can apply only where there is no merit, or it is not mercy.

The one who has received mercy will be merciful. The one who has received forgiveness will be forgiving. If you are a merciful person, you give evidence of being God's child; so every time you sin, God forgives. Every time you have a need, He meets it. He takes care of you. He just pours mercy upon mercy upon mercy to those who show mercy, because they have received it from the merciful God.

Are you merciful? — John MacArthur, *The Beatitudes: The Only Way to Happiness* (Chicago: Moody Press, 1998).

15. Verse 8. Sometimes, the best way to understand what the Bible means is to think about the opposite. What is the opposite of being pure in heart? What do we not want to be like?

Sometimes on festive occasions we wear costumes and masks to celebrate in a special way. We wear these masks for three reasons:

1.   So we can pretend to be something we are not.

2.   So we can disguise who we really are.

3.   So we can separate ourselves from everybody else.

Where I grew up, we used to call these masks false faces. We wear masks for parties and celebrations, but for some people mask-wearing is an everyday affair. They wear "false faces" continually—pretending to be something they are not, trying to disguise who they really are, setting themselves apart from everybody else.

When Jesus came into the world, he saw people wearing masks, and it bothered him. Of course, the most notorious "mask-wearers" of Jesus' day were the religious leaders— the Pharisees and the Sadducees. They wore the mask of outward purity, a mask that said to everybody, "Look at me! See how clean and pure and godly I am. See my good works! Aren't you impressed? See how I keep the Law. Don't come too near me now, for I am holier-than-thou!"

But all that pompous, pious talk, was like a false face, an artificial appearance. They looked good outwardly, but inwardly, their hearts were made of stone. They talked loudly of goodness, but they kicked sand in the faces of the hurting people around them. They kept the letter of the Law, but missed the message of mercy and love. They were so busy holding their "I'm better than you" mask in place, they had no time or energy left over for compassion.

Jesus saw right through their pretensions and disguises, and he had strong words for them: "Woe to you, scribes and

Pharisees, hypocrites! For you are like whitewashed tombs, which . . . inside are full of the bones of the dead" (Matt. 23:27). Those are tough words, to be sure, but Jesus wanted to emphasize dramatically the importance of the inner life. It's what's inside that counts! That's what he says in this sixth Beatitude: "Blessed are the pure in heart, for they will see God."

In other words: Don't be pretentious! Don't be fake.Don't be artificial! Don't be holier-than-thou! Don't be hypocritical! Don't make a show of religion and miss the message! Be genuine and honest and real within.Give God your heart. — James W. Moore, *When All Else Fails Read the Instructions* (Nashville: Abingdon Press, 2011).

16. Verse 9. Why is peacemaking such a difficult work?

THE PROBLEM of human strife is as old as man. It had its beginning on the outskirts of Eden when Cain, driven by envy, murdered his more devout brother, Abel. Men fought then as now: primarily because strife was inherent in their natures.

Jesus spoke prophetically of our times when He said: "And ye shall hear of wars and rumors of wars . . . nation shall rise against nation, and kingdom against kingdom . . ." (Matthew 24:6–7).

Someone has pointed out that over the past 4,000 years there have been fewer than 300 years of peace. Yet one wonders, was that universal peace? It is more likely that down through history there has always been a war, or wars, in various parts of the world. Even the most optimistic person is forced to admit that there is something seriously wrong with a world that has such a passion for destruction.

If a man were sent from Mars to report earth's major business, he would in all fairness have to say that war was the earth's chief industry. He would report that the nations of the world were vying with each other in a race to see which could make deadlier weapons and amass bigger nuclear arsenals. He would say that earth's people are too quarrelsome to get along with each other and too selfish to live peacefully together. — Billy Graham, *The Secret of Happiness* (Nashville: Thomas Nelson, 2002).

17. What is the key to being a good peacemaker?

Peacemaking is a noble vocation. But you can no more make peace in your own strength than a mason can build a wall without a trowel, a carpenter build a house without a hammer, or an artist paint a picture without a brush. You must have the proper equipment. To be a peacemaker, you must know the Peace-Giver. To make peace on earth, you must know the peace of heaven. You must know Him who "is our peace."

Jesus didn't leave a material inheritance to His disciples. All He had when He died was a robe, which went to the Roman soldiers; His mother, whom He turned over to His brother John; His body, which He gave to Joseph of Arimathea; and His Spirit, which returned to His Father.

But Jesus willed His followers something more valuable than gold, more enduring than vast landholdings and more to be desired than palaces of marble—He willed us His peace. He said: "My peace I give unto you: not as the world giveth, give I unto you. Let not your heart be troubled, neither let it be afraid" (John 14:27).

Only as we know Him and the peace He imparts can we be peacemakers . . . and He promised happiness to a maker of peace!

The key is commitment to become peacemakers—to be men and women who actively seek to bring the peace of Christ to others and to our world. — Billy Graham, *The Secret of Happiness* (Nashville: Thomas Nelson, 2002).

18. Blessed are the persecuted. Have you seen persecution in real life today? Who has a story? What kind of persecution do Christians experience today?

Jenny Adams serves in Peru as a missionary with Baptist Mid-Missions. She has been there for 34 years, ministering faithfully as a teacher at the mission's Bible school and in several remote villages. She drove her own van and often gave passengers rides into town. One day she offered a ride to a young woman who had previously attended the mission school, the daughter of a village pastor. Little did Miss Adams know that this young woman's brother was a cocaine processor who frequently used his sister to transport the drugs. Miss Adams was arrested with more than 3 kilos of cocaine in her vehicle, and under Peruvian law a person is guilty until proven innocent. In her case, the press was quick to exploit the story to discredit foreign missionaries. The newspapers dubbed her "the cocaine missionary," and her long years of service were ignored. After 20 days of imprisonment, Jenny Adams was released, but not until the work of her mission had suffered from false witnesses. She was innocent of all charges, but that didn't matter. She was persecuted anyway. — David Jeremiah, *How to Be Happy according to Jesus: Study Guide* (Nashville, TN: Thomas Nelson Publishers, 1996), 102.

19. Summary. How does Jesus' path to happiness differ from the world's path?

A distraught, miserable man was looking for help and sought the counsel of a liberal minister. Looking at the unhappy condition of the man, the minister said, "Forget about those things. Go and see this famous comedian that is appearing at a local comedy club. I hear that he is keeping everyone in stitches. Go listen to him, and you will forget how miserable you feel." After a moment of silence, the man said, "I am that comedian."

What is happiness? I think the world's version of it is quite different than the Bible's version. The happiness of this world depends on circumstances. If you are in good health, the bills are paid, and things are going well, then according to the world's philosophy, you are happy. But if someone cuts you off on the freeway or if something else goes wrong, then suddenly you are unhappy. Your happiness hinges on what is happening at a given moment.

The Bible gives us a completely different view of this thing called happiness. According to Scripture, true happiness is never something that should be sought directly; it always results from seeking something else. When we are trying to be happy, when we are trying to be fulfilled, we rarely are. But when we forget about those things and get back to the very purpose for which God put us on the earth, suddenly we find the wonderful byproduct of happiness popping up in our lives. When we seek holiness, we will find happiness. When we seek righteousness, we will become happy people, because our will is aligned with the will of God as we walk in harmony with Him. The rest of our lives will then find their proper balance. — Greg Laurie, *For Every Season: Daily Devotions* (Dana Point, CA: Kerygma Publishing—Allen David Books, 2011).

20. How can we support one another in prayer this week?

The third "one another" is "pray for one another" (James 5:16). This responsibility is at the heart of relationships in the Body. It is something no Christian can avoid and still be a contributing member of the Body. Such mutual prayer is based on the honest sharing of personal needs and the personal discipline involved in setting aside a regular time for it. — John MacArthur Jr., *The Body Dynamic* (Colorado Springs, CO: Chariot Victor Publishing, 1996), 124.

Lesson #6, Matthew 6.5 - 18
Good Questions Have Groups Talking
www.joshhunt.com

Matthew 6.5 - 18

OPEN

Let's each share your name and one thing you find yourself praying for these days.

DIG

1. **Today, we will be talking about Jesus' teaching on prayer. To get us started, let's talk a bit about our experience in prayer. What is your practice in prayer? What do you love about prayer? What frustrates you about prayer?**

    Often when we pray for others, we either fall into meaningless repetition, or submit a grocery list of requests to God, hoping that He'll respond to our wishes and desires. When we've finished praying, we end up being unsatisfied, fretful, and uncertain as to whether or not we can trust God with the assignment we've just given Him.

    My personal experience has been that such "need-based" praying is often boring, filled with uncertainty, and reduces prayer to a meaningless exercise.

    What if we changed our perspective on prayer and began to pray Scripture? What if we echoed back to God that which we know is His will? Wouldn't that stimulate our faith, bring glory to Him, and rid us of the repetition that Jesus warned us about when He said, "When you are praying, do not use meaningless repetition"(Matthew 6:7)?

Years ago I discovered that when I pray Scripture, I anticipate my time of prayer with excitement, wondering exactly what I would pray next. Best of all, praying in this way sinks deep roots into God's promises and His will. Such prayer is effective not just in moving God's heart toward us, but in giving us a deep and settled satisfaction of knowing that we've just connected with our heavenly Father.

Will you join me in praying Scripture for ourselves and others? — Erwin Lutzer, *Covering Your Life in Prayer: Discover a Life-Changing Conversation with God* (Eugene, OR: Harvest House, 2013).

2. Is prayer hard? Is prayer complicated?

As you've just read in Before Amen: The Power of a Simple Prayer, many of the prayers in the Bible can be distilled to a few clear and memorable lines. A powerful, life-changing conversation with God can begin here:

Father,

you are good.

I need help. Heal me and forgive me.

They need help.

Thank you.

In Jesus' name, amen.

Max Lucado*, Before Amen: The Power of a Simple Prayer* (Nashville: Thomas Nelson, 2014).

3. Matthew 5.6. Notice the opening line, "When you pray..." Was Jesus addressing a praying people?

NO nation ever had a higher ideal of prayer than the Jews had; and no religion ever ranked prayer higher in the scale of priorities than the Jews did. 'Great is prayer,' said the Rabbis, 'greater than all good works.' One of the loveliest things that was ever said about family worship is the Rabbinic saying: 'He who prays within his house surrounds it with a wall that is stronger than iron.' The only regret of the Rabbis was that it was not possible to pray all day long.

But certain faults had crept into the Jewish habits of prayer. It is to be noted that these faults are by no means peculiar to Jewish ideas of prayer; they can and do occur anywhere. And it is to be noted that they could only occur in a community where prayer was taken with the greatest seriousness. They are not the faults of neglect; they are the faults of misguided devotion.

(1) Prayer tended to become formalized. There were two things the daily use of which was prescribed for every Jew.

The first was the Shema, which consists of three short passages of Scripture—Deuteronomy 6:4–9, 11:13–21; Numbers 15:37–41. Shema is the imperative of the Hebrew word for to hear, and the Shema takes its name from the verse which was the essence and centre of the whole matter: 'Hear, O Israel, the Lord our God is one Lord.'

The full Shema had to be recited by every Jew every morning and every evening. It had to be said as early as possible. It had to be said as soon as the light was strong enough to distinguish between blue and white, or, as Rabbi Eliezer said, between blue and green. In any event, it had to be said before the third hour, that is, 9 am; and in the evening it had to be said before 9 pm. If the last possible moment for the saying of the Shema had come, no matter where a man found himself, at home, in the street, at work or in the synagogue, he must stop and say it.

There were many who loved the Shema, and who repeated it with reverence and adoration and love; but inevitably there were still more who gabbled their way through it and went their way. The Shema had every chance of becoming a vain repetition, which was mumbled like some incantation. We Christians are but ill-qualified to criticize, for everything that has been said about formally gabbling through the Shema can be said about grace before meals in many families.

The second thing which every Jew had to repeat daily was called the Shemonēh 'esreh, which means the Eighteen. It consisted of eighteen prayers, and was, and still is, an essential part of the synagogue service. In time the prayers became nineteen, but the old name remains. Most of these prayers are quite short, and nearly all of them are very lovely.

The twelfth runs:

> Let Thy mercy, O Lord, be showed upon the upright, the humble, the elders of thy people Israel, and the rest of its teachers; be favourable to the pious strangers among us, and to us all. Give thou a good reward to those who sincerely trust in thy name, that our lot may be cast among them in the world to come, that our hope be not deceived. Praised be thou, O Lord, who art the hope and confidence of the faithful.

The fifth runs:

> Bring us back to thy law, O our Father; bring us back, O King, to thy service; bring us back to thee by true repentance. Praised be thou, O Lord, who dost accept our repentance.

No church possesses a more beautiful liturgy than the Shemonēh 'esreh. The law was that Jews must recite it three times a day—once in the morning, once in the afternoon and once in the evening. The same thing happened again. Devout Jews prayed it with loving devotion; but there were many to whom this series of lovely prayers became a gabbled formula. There was even a summary supplied which might be prayed, if there was not the time to repeat the whole eighteen or they could not all be remembered. The repetition of the Shemonēh 'esreh became nothing more than a superstitious incantation. Again, we Christians are ill-qualified to criticize, for there are many occasions when we do precisely the same with the prayer which Christ taught us to pray. — William Barclay, *The Gospel of Matthew, Third Ed., The New Daily Study Bible* (Edinburgh: Saint Andrew Press, 2001), 220–222.

4. How would you summarize Jesus' message in verse 5 – 8?

The Pharisees designated the third hour, the sixth hour, and the ninth hour as times of prayer. In other words, at nine o'clock in the morning, at noon, and at three o'clock in the afternoon, they would faithfully gather in the synagogues or in the temple to offer their prayers. We are told in the Book of Daniel that he, a man of God, opened his windows toward Jerusalem and prayed three times a day. But the Pharisees were not doing it to seek the Lord, but rather to be seen by men. How do we know this? On their way to prayer meetings, the Pharisees would stop on the corner of the street and begin to offer long and verbose prayers. In so doing, they were saying, "We are so eager to pray, we can't wait to get to the synagogue."

And people would say, "Oh, wow! Look how righteous they are!"

We still do that in our own subtle ways, don't we? "Yes, as I was praying this morning at three o'clock, the Lord brought you to my heart." And we subtly let people know we are in a place of continual prayer. Jesus said, "Don't do it. That's hypocrisy." — Jon Courson, *Jon Courson's Application Commentary* (Nashville, TN: Thomas Nelson, 2003), 31.

5. Verse 6. Is Jesus teaching against public prayers?

We must pray in secret before we pray in public (v. 6). It is not wrong to pray in public in the assembly (1 Tim. 2:1ff), or even when blessing food (John 6:11) or seeking God's help (John 11:41-42; Acts 27:35). But it is wrong to pray in public if we are not in the habit of praying in private. Observers may think that we are practicing prayer when we are not, and this is hypocrisy. The word translated closet means "a private chamber." It could refer to the store-chamber in a house. Our Lord prayed privately (Mark 1:35); so did Elisha (2 Kings 4:32ff) and Daniel (Dan. 6:10ff). — *Bible Exposition Commentary (BE Series) - New Testament - The Bible Exposition Commentary – New Testament, Volume 1.*

6. Verse 7. Is repetition in prayer a good thing or a bad thing?

The fact that a request is repeated does not make it a "vain repetition"; for both Jesus and Paul repeated their petitions (Matt. 26:36-46; 2 Cor. 12:7-8). A request becomes a "vain repetition" if it is only a babbling of words without a sincere heart desire to seek and do God's will. The mere reciting of memorized prayers can be vain repetition. The Gentiles had such prayers in their pagan ceremonies (see 1 Kings 18:26).

My friend Dr. Robert A. Cook has often said, "All of us have one routine prayer in our system; and once we get rid of it, then we can really start to pray!" I have noticed this, not only in my own praying, but often when I have conducted prayer meetings. With some people, praying is like putting the needle on a phonograph record and then forgetting about it. But God does not answer insincere prayers. — *Bible Exposition Commentary (BE Series) - New Testament - The Bible Exposition Commentary – New Testament, Volume 1.*

7. Verse 8. If God already knows everything, why do we need to tell Him in prayer?

We are not to act like the heathen who think they have to help God hear their prayers by praying long, repetitive prayers. We do not pray to inform God—He already knows what we need before we ask Him. We pray in order to fellowship with Him and discern His will. We, not God, are changed by our prayers. Even with regard to our daily needs, Jesus says, "Your heavenly Father knows that you need all these things" (Matthew 6:32).

The fact that God already knows our needs immediately raises the question, "Why, then, pray at all?" More than any other reason, we pray out of obedience—God has commanded us to pray.

But there are other reasons as well. Sometimes we think we know what we need, but our heavenly Father knows what we really need. Sometimes He changes our heart about what we're asking for while we're praying. Since God knows all things actual and possible, it is a comfort to know that He can tell us what we need instead of us having to tell Him what we need. Also, prayer brings us into submission to the will of God. As we pray, the Spirit of God is at work in us to conform our wills to the will of God. Most Christians will readily admit they are glad God has not answered all their prayers. He knows what we need better than we do. — David Jeremiah, *Knowing the God You Worship: Study Guide* (Nashville, TN: Thomas Nelson Publishers, 2004), 82.

8. Is the purpose of prayer to change God's mind?

Prayer is not conquering God's reluctance to answer, but laying hold of His willingness to help us! Prayer, in the life of the true believer, is an act of total confidence and assurance in the plan and purpose of God who is ever cognizant, ever knowing of our needs. We do not need to pray lengthy, vain prayers because Jesus' disciples do not need to inform their omniscient Father of their needs in prayer. He already knows what they are.

Why pray then? It is the basis of our communicating with God. Prayer is not designed to inform God, but to give man a sight of his own weakness; to humble his heart, to excite his desire, to inflame his faith, to animate his hope, to raise his soul from earth to Heaven, and to put him in mind that God is God. More than changing things, prayer changes people. Essentially we pray for the same reasons children speak to their parents. We are to share our concerns, to have fellowship, to obtain help, and to express our gratitude to the Lord. Prayer keeps our heart soft, tender, and at peace. This is how it changes us. In prayer, we acknowledge our need and dependence upon the Lord. We also pray because God does things in answer to prayer that He would not have done otherwise. — *Mattoon's Treasures – Treasures from The Sermon on the Mount, Volume 2.*

9. Who can tell of a time when God answered your prayer? Who has a story?

In his book, Say It With Love, Howard Hendricks recorded this true story about answered prayer: We had a lovely couple in

Dallas a number of years ago. He sold his business at a loss, went into vocational Christian work, and things got rather rough. There were four kids in the family. One night at family worship, Timmy, the youngest boy, said, "Daddy, do you think Jesus would mind if I asked Him for a shirt?" "Well, no, of course not. Let's write that down in our prayer request book, Mother." So she wrote down "shirt for Timmy" and she added "size seven."

You can be sure that every day Timmy saw to it that they prayed for the shirt. After several weeks, one Saturday the mother received a telephone call from a clothier in downtown Dallas, a Christian businessman. "I've just finished my July clearance sale and knowing that you have four boys it occurred to me that you might use something we have left. Could you use some boy's shirts?" She said, "What size?" "Size seven." "How many do you have?" she asked hesitantly. He said, "Twelve." Many of us might have taken the shirts, stuffed them in the bureau drawer, and made some casual comment to the child. Not this wise set of parents.

That night, as expected, Timmy said, "Don't forget, Mommy, let's pray for the shirt." Mommy said, "We don't have to pray for the shirt, Timmy," "How come?" "The Lord has answered your prayer." "He has?" "Right." So, as previously arranged, brother Tommy goes out and gets one shirt, brings it in, and puts it down on the table. Little Timmy's eyes are like saucers. Tommy goes out and gets another shirt and brings it in. Out—back, out—back, until he piles 12 shirts on the table, and Timmy thinks God is going into the shirt business. But you know, there is a little kid in Dallas today by the name of Timothy who believes there is a God in Heaven interested enough in his needs to provide little boys with shirts. Thank God, He answers our prayers. — *Mattoon's Treasures – Treasures from The Sermon on the Mount, Volume 2.*

10. Verse 9ff. Notice the pronouns in this prayer. You might circle them. What do we learn about prayer from this?

It is worth noting that there are no singular pronouns in this prayer; they are all plural. It begins with "OUR Father."

When we pray, we must remember that we are part of God's worldwide family of believers. We have no right to ask for ourselves anything that would harm another member of the family. If we are praying in the will of God, the answer will be a blessing to all of God's people in one way or another.
— *Bible Exposition Commentary (BE Series) - New Testament - The Bible Exposition Commentary – New Testament, Volume 1.*

11. Jesus taught us to pray beginning with the word "Father." What does that teach us about prayer?

"Abba! Father! "You probably know that many scholars believe the Aramaic word Abba equates to the affectionate name we know today as Daddy. Understand this as the radical statement it was—and is!

Jesus spoke to His Father the way we would speak to our dads—in the tender, trusting, respectful manner you know is good, even if it doesn't mirror your own personal experience with your earthly father. He talked to Him simply, openly, honestly, securely, without any reservation or hesitation.

And by teaching His disciples to pray in this way, Jesus was authorizing them to share His sonship, to relate to the sovereign God of the universe with the intimacy of a child climbing up in his daddy's lap, throwing his arms around his neck, and telling him, "I love You."

This is not irreverence; it is relationship. And to the first-century mind, it was absolutely revolutionary. — Kenneth S. Hemphill and Ken Hemphill, *The Prayer of Jesus: The Promise and Power of Living in the Lord's Prayer* (Nashville: B&H, 2001).

12. What does the opening word (Father) teach us about God Himself?

My girls are grown now. Two are off and married; one is away at college. But even now, when I think about them or hear one of their voices on the phone, I get a lump in my throat. I love them so much.

I cannot imagine a time when I would be too busy to help them or would brush them off if they needed something from me. When one of my girls calls and asks for something that I know is good and important to them, I do everything in my power to ensure they get it. I rejoice in their accomplishments, support them in their dreams and endeavors, and take a hundred times more pleasure in their successes than in any of my own.

I keep their pictures in my wallet. I know their mailing addresses and phone numbers in my head. If you were to visit my office today, you would see a crayon-etched diploma inscribed to the "World's Best Dad" hanging right along with the official university diplomas and other awards I have received.

When my girls hurt, I feel their pain.

When they cry, I weep right along with them.

When they struggle, I lie awake at night thinking about them.

Is there any doubt our Father will do any less? Doesn't this knowledge alone make you want to come into His presence and stay there throughout the day? — Kenneth S. Hemphill and Ken Hemphill, *The Prayer of Jesus: The Promise and Power of Living in the Lord's Prayer* (Nashville: B&H, 2001).

13. Verse 10. What exactly does it mean, "Your kingdom come..."?

When we pray, "hallowed be your name, your kingdom come," we are praying that this world will be made holy, like heaven. We are praying that every power not of God will be turned over and every human empire destroyed. Read the news and you will see that God is turning over empires right now. God will have only one kingdom. Jesus alerts us to the signs that his kingdom is coming: earthquakes, wars and rumors of war, hearts growing cold. Right now he is getting ready for his final kingdom.

God has equipped us well to live in this world. We are a holy temple. Christ dwells in us by the Holy Spirit. The Spirit teaches us the meaning of the cross. He convicts the world of sin and unbelief. When people know they are sinners and know they need a Savior, then the door is open for the kingdom of God to come in and change everything. Keep on asking for the Spirit—for yourself and for the world. — C. John Miller and Rose Marie Miller, *Saving Grace: Daily Devotions from Jack Miller* (Greensboro, NC: New Growth Press, 2014).

14. Let's focus just a bit more. What is a kingdom?

This vision of the kingdom is where Jesus started and where we must also start. He came announcing, manifesting, and teaching the availability and nature of the kingdom of the heavens. "For I was sent for this purpose," he said (Luke 4:43).

The kingdom of God is the range of God's effective will, where what God wants done is done. Earth and its immediate surroundings seem to be the only place in creation where God permits his will to not be done. Therefore we pray, "Thy kingdom come, Thy will be done in earth, as it is in heaven" (Matthew 6:10, KJV) and hope for the time when that kingdom will be completely fulfilled even here on earth, where, in fact, it is already present (see Luke 17:21) and available to those who seek it with all their heart (see Matthew 6:33; 11:12; Luke 16:16). For those who seek it, it is true even now that all things work together for their good and that nothing can cut them off from God's inseparable love and effective care (see Romans 8:28, 35–39).

The vision that underlies spiritual transformation into Christlikeness is, then, the vision of life now and forever in the range of God's effective will, that is, partaking of the divine nature through a birth "from above" and participating by our actions in what God is doing now in our lifetime on earth (see 2 Peter 1:4, 1 John 3:1–2). Therefore, we can say, "Whatever we do, speaking or acting, we do all on behalf of the Lord Jesus, giving thanks through him to God the Father" (Colossians 3:17, PAR). In everything we do, we are permitted to do his work. What we are aiming for in this vision is to live fully in the kingdom of God, as fully as possible now and here, not just hereafter. — Dallas Willard and Jan Johnson, *Renovation of the Heart in Daily Practice: Experiments in Spiritual Transformation* (Colorado Springs, CO: NavPress, 2006), 57–58.

15. How important was the topic of the kingdom of God to Jesus' teaching?

The first day Dallas asked the class, "What was the gospel, or good news, of Jesus?" The students, most of them pastors, began saying things like, "Jesus came and died for our sins so that we can go to heaven when we die," or something close to that. After a while there was silence, and Dallas said forcefully, "No. That was not Jesus' good news. His good news was about the availability of the kingdom of God." I could see the disbelief on their faces, and if I had had a mirror I would have seen it on mine. Dallas went on that entire morning teaching directly from the Gospels and Acts, walking us through passage after passage, wearing us down with the truth that had been right in front of us all the time, but we had missed it. Every one of us was a seminary graduate, and we had missed the most fundamental aspect of ministry. — Gary W. Moon, John Ortberg, et al., *Eternal Living: Reflections on Dallas Willard's Teaching on Faith and Formation* (Westmont, IL: InterVarsity Press, 2015).

16. What does verse 11 teach us about God?

Give us today our daily bread'" (Matt. 6:9, 11). God provides us with everything we need. But there are times when that provision doesn't come as quickly as we'd like.

Have you ever been in a situation where you had no food to eat or no money to pay your bills? I have. Maybe you're in such a situation right now and don't know where to turn. Having walked with the Lord for more than thirty years, I can tell you God has always provided for my needs, as Philippians 4:19 promises: "And my God will meet all your needs according to his glorious riches in Christ Jesus." Notice this doesn't say God will supply all our greeds. But it does say that

God will provide for all our needs. Yet so often, we struggle to believe God will do so. — Greg Laurie, *Walking with Jesus: Daily Inspiration from the Gospel of John* (Grand Rapids, MI: Baker, 2007).

17. Verse 11. Do you think God ever gets tired of us asking for stuff?

First, God commands us to ask. Jesus told two parables that illustrate this point. One was about an unexpected guest who dropped in on a man and his family one night, catching them without enough food in the house to set before him. His host, though he knew the hour was late, crept out at midnight to the home of a friend, knocked on the door, and asked him for three loaves of bread. Roused from sleep, the neighbor at first showed reluctance to get out of bed, but— Jesus finishes the story—"even though he will not get up and give him anything because he is his friend, yet because of his persistence he will get up and give him as much as he needs" (Luke 11:8).

The second parable tells the story of a widow who repeatedly appealed to a local judge for legal protection against someone who was threatening her. For a good while the judge who did not fear God and did not respect man continued to put her off and dismiss her claim. But at last he relented. "Otherwise by continually coming she will wear me out" (Luke 18:5).

It's clear, then, that Jesus has instructed us not only to ask but to persist in asking.

> "Ask, and it will be given to you; seek, and you will find; knock, and it will be opened to you. For everyone who asks receives, and he who seeks finds; and to him who knocks it will be opened." (Matt. 7:7–8)

The characters in Jesus' stories were in need, but they knew exactly where to go for help. Were it not for the humble task of asking, the man would have had to send his tired guest to bed hungry. Were it not for the courage of daily perseverance, the widow might have lost all her possessions to a ruthless opponent. They both exercised their dependence on one who had the power and authority to help them, and they both received as much as they needed from his hand.

Since we know that our Father gives good gifts to His children, we should continue to pray—even when we don't get an answer the first day—so that we are not tempted to try to get our needs met somewhere else. — Kenneth S. Hemphill and Ken Hemphill, *The Prayer of Jesus: The Promise and Power of Living in the Lord's Prayer* (Nashville: B&H, 2001).

18. Verse 12. Doesn't God forgive all our sins—past, present and future—when we are saved? Why do we need to continually ask for forgiveness?

One kind of forgiveness to which Jesus is calling us in Matthew 6 and 18 is what I call "relational forgiveness." An illustration might help to explain what I mean.

When I was a teenager, I was fascinated with the idea of driving long before I was legally allowed to drive. One day my father left his Chrysler sitting in the driveway. He tempted me—he put the keys on the table. Nobody was home. I decided this was my opportunity to take that car out for a spin.

I didn't want to motor down a highly traveled street, so I found a gravel road out in the country. I was tooling along when I saw a farmer in his truck approaching me. He decided to take his half of the lane out of the middle and flat ran me off the road! Now I had my dad's new Chrysler in the ditch, and I freaked out. I thought about running away from home. I thought about suicide.

Finally a guy pulled me out with his tractor. Somehow I got that car home, complete with one side all smashed up. If I remember correctly, I had to keep turning left; I couldn't turn right. Somehow I got the thing in the driveway and waited for the inevitable. I died a thousand deaths in those hours while I waited for my dad to come home.

I was watching through the window when he arrived. He stood and stared at the car, shook his head, walked in and asked, "David, did you do that?"

"Yeah, I did."

He shook his head again. My dad normally responded in a more forceful way. This time he just kept shaking his head and walked into the other room. He didn't talk. Not at supper, not at breakfast, not at lunch, not at supper the next night. O, it was awful!

Finally it hit me: This was my fault. I had to fix this. So, I went to see him at work and said, "Dad, I've got to tell you I feel terrible about what I did. I was wrong, deceitful, dishonest. I knew better than to do that. I'm sorry, and I want to ask you to forgive me."

"You're forgiven," he said. "And you will pay for the car."

Now, when I wrecked my dad's car, did I cease to be my father's son? No. But our working relationship was in deep trouble. In order to be restored, I had to ask forgiveness for my actions and my dad had to extend it. I had to repent, and true repentance required paying for the car.

If we want to know oneness with the Lord in our daily relationship with Him, if we want to feel a closeness when we pray to God, we can't hold grudges against others. If we did, how could we come to God and say, "Father, I just love being forgiven, and itwonderful to talk to you"? The Bible clearly says that if we come to the altar and remember that someone has something against us, or if we have something against someone else, we must go find our brother, be reconciled to him, and only then come back and talk to God.
— David Jeremiah, *Prayer: The Great Adventure* (Sisters, OR: Multnomah Publishers, 1997), 143–145.

19. Is forgiving others really a condition of being forgiven?

Jesus does not question the reality of your wounds. He does not doubt that you have been sinned against. The issue is not the existence of pain; the issue is the treatment of pain. What are you going to do with your debts?

Dale Carnegie tells about a visit to Yellowstone Park, where he saw a grizzly bear. The huge animal was in the center of a clearing, feeding on some discarded camp food. For several minutes he feasted alone; no other creature dared draw near. After a few moments a skunk walked through the meadow toward the food and took his place next to the grizzly. The bear didn't object, and Carnegie knew why. "The grizzly," he said, "knew the high cost of getting even."

We'd be wise to learn the same. Settling the score is done at great expense. — Max Lucado, *For the Tough Times: Reaching toward Heaven for Hope* (Nashville: Thomas Nelson, 2008).

20. Summarize. What does the Bible teach about prayer—in this passage, and elsewhere?

I don't mean I had trouble finding an item or two; I mean I found nothing. Everything God does in the work of ministry, He does through prayer. Consider:

- Prayer is the way you defeat the devil (Luke 22:32; James 4:7).

- Prayer is the way you get the lost saved (Luke 18:13).

- Prayer is the way you acquire wisdom (James 1:5).

- Prayer is the way a backslider gets restored (James 5:16–20).

- Prayer is how the saints get strengthened (Jude 20, Matthew 26:41).

- Prayer is the way we get laborers out to the mission field (Matthew 9:38).

- Prayer is how we cure the sick (James 5:13–15).

- Prayer is how we accomplish the impossible (Mark 11:23–24).

David Jeremiah, *Prayer: The Great Adventure* (Sisters, OR: Multnomah Publishers, 1997), 40–41.

21. How can we support one another in prayer this week?

This kind of prayer is usually referred to as intercessory prayer. It has the wonderful benefit of enlarging our hearts toward others, as well as taking our focus off ourselves. And intercessory prayer is one of the ways God prefers to accomplish His will. He wants our prayers to be the tools He uses to bring healing, provision, and hope into the lives of others. When we intercede for others, we carry in our heart their burdens so that they need not carry them alone. Praying for someone is a way of loving them.

Think about the people in your life who have needs and burdens. Will you commit yourself to praying for them? Perhaps it would be good to keep a running list of prayer requests. As you find a few moments, pray for the people on your list. Then, once in a while, check in with them to see if they still need you to keep praying or if they just need the encouragement of knowing that someone is dedicated to praying for them for the long haul. I have people for whom I have been praying for many years. My regular prayers for them knit our hearts together and deepen our relationships, even when I don't see them as often as I would like. Intercessory prayer is the glue that binds us together. — Terry Glaspey, *25 Keys to Life-Changing Prayer* (Eugene, OR: Harvest House, 2010).

Lesson #7, Matthew 5.17 – 45
Good Questions Have Groups Talking
www.joshhunt.com

Matthew 5.17 – 22; 43 - 45

OPEN

Let's each share your name and one thing you are grateful for.

DIG

1. **Matthew 5.17 – 22. Summarize Jesus' teaching in this passage?**

   He is pro-Old Testament. In fact, to Jesus the smallest letter (i.e., the Hebrew letter yod) and the least stroke of a pen (i.e., a horn—the ornamental marks customarily added to certain Hebrew letters) matter to Jesus. None of what Jesus is saying and doing is abolishing any word, letter, or mark that has been written. He is not relaxing or teaching anyone to relax any of God's commands. Rather, he is living out and teaching others to live out those very rules. And while he has been or will be dining with sinners, talking with women, healing on the Sabbath, and even overturning the greedy and racist moneychangers' tables in the temple, none of those things are aberrations of God's Word, as the scribes and Pharisees think. Instead those actions accord with the Law's highest principles. — Douglas Sean O'Donnell, *Matthew: All Authority in Heaven and on Earth, ed. R. Kent Hughes, Preaching the Word* (Wheaton, IL: Crossway, 2013), 128.

2. Look over the Sermon on the Mount as a whole. How does this part fit in the context?

The Law or the Prophets was one way of referring to the entire Hebrew Scriptures (our Old Testament). Jesus meant the same thing in 5:18 when he referred to the Law. Jesus was about to say some things that would strike the minds of the religious leaders like a sledgehammer. He would sound to their ears as though he were antilaw because he would insist the law can do nothing for them except define sin. It cannot save them even if they could (hypothetically) keep it perfectly (exceeding the Pharisees). So Jesus assured his Jewish listeners that he was not antilaw at all. On the contrary, he was going to fulfill it; that is, both keep and explain fully its original intention, which they had managed to miss over the centuries. — Stuart K. Weber, Matthew, vol. 1, Holman New Testament Commentary (Nashville, TN: Broadman & Holman Publishers, 2000), 63.

3. Look at verse 18 in several translations. What was the least stroke of the pen?

The least stroke (5:18) of the Hebrew alphabet is the yod. It is no bigger than our apostrophe. The smallest stroke of a pen is a very tiny mark that is only one part of a single Hebrew letter, like the dot over our "i." Jesus was serious about the eternal quality of his written Word. We must never trifle with even the smallest part of Scripture. Jesus affirmed the inerrancy of Scripture and its absolute trustworthiness. — Stuart K. Weber, *Matthew, vol. 1, Holman New Testament Commentary* (Nashville, TN: Broadman & Holman Publishers, 2000), 64.

4. What does it mean to fulfil the law? If you have a Study Bible, there may be a note.

Jesus was essentially declaring war on the false pharisaical religion. He insisted that no person could be saved by his or her own righteousness. This was something the law intended to indicate all along, but Israel had missed the point (Rom. 2:17–3:31; Gal. 3:17–29; 5:3–6). The point was hard for the self-righteous to swallow—no one, not even the super law-keeping Pharisees, could enter into heaven. All needed a Savior! — Stuart K. Weber, *Matthew, vol. 1, Holman New Testament Commentary* (Nashville, TN: Broadman & Holman Publishers, 2000), 65.

5. Verse 20 doesn't move us much. How would it have felt to the original hearers?

This statement would have shocked those who heard it because, according to a popular Jewish saying of the time, "If only two men made it into heaven, one would be a scribe, and the other a Pharisee." The scribes were scholars who studied, interpreted, and commented endlessly upon the Law. The word "pharisee" literally means "separated one." Numbering seven thousand, this company of men kept the minutest details of the Law.

We look at the scribes and Pharisees rather humorously today, but no one did then. They were the Billy Grahams, Chuck Swindolls, and Jack Hayfords—the spiritual giants of their day. And Jesus said even their righteousness wasn't good enough. — Jon Courson, *Jon Courson's Application Commentary* (Nashville, TN: Thomas Nelson, 2003), 27.

6. Matthew 5.43 – 45. Summarize Jesus' teaching in this passage?

These verses develop the idea of loving one's enemies by first comparing such love to God's love for people (5:45) and then by asking two rhetorical questions that call on disciples to practice a higher righteousness than tax collectors and pagans do (5:46–47).

Corrupt tax collectors. (NLT) "Corrupt" refers to the practices of "tax farmers," who paid the Romans for the right to collect taxes and then collected more than was due, keeping the overage for themselves. When Jews sometimes became "tax farmers," they were regarded as thieves and traitors, which may explain Jesus' pairing of tax collectors (5:46) with pagans (5:47; cf. 18:17). For Jesus' association with tax collectors, see 9:9–11; 11:19; 21:31–32; Luke 18:9–14; 19:1–10.

It is clear that action, not emotion, is called for here, since disciples are not only to pray for enemies (5:44) but also to do them good, as God does (5:45; cf. Ps 145:9; Luke 6:35; Acts 14:17), and to greet them respectfully (5:47). This last action may imply a wish for their welfare (Gen 43:27; Exod 18:7 LXX). — David Turner and Darrell L. Bock, *Cornerstone Biblical Commentary, Vol 11: Matthew and Mark* (Carol Stream, IL: Tyndale House Publishers, 2005), 94.

7. Think over the life of Jesus. How did He practice what He taught?

What would it mean to reflect God's generous love despite the pressure and provocation, despite your own anger and frustration?

Impossible? Well, yes, at one level. But again Jesus' teaching isn't just good advice, it's good news. Jesus did it all himself, and opened up the new way of being human so that all who follow him can discover it. When they mocked him, he didn't respond. When they challenged him, he told quizzical, sometimes humorous, stories that forced them to think differently. When they struck him, he took the pain. When they put the worst bit of Roman equipment on his back—the heavy cross-piece on which he would be killed—he carried it out of the city to the place of his own execution. When they nailed him to the cross, he prayed for them. — Tom Wright, *Matthew for Everyone, Part 1: Chapters 1-15* (London: Society for Promoting Christian Knowledge, 2004), 52–53.

8. How was Jesus' own life blessed by following this teaching?

In spite of experiencing misunderstanding, ingratitude, and rejection, our Lord never became bitter, discouraged, or overcome. Every obstacle was an opportunity. Brokenheartedness? An opportunity to comfort. Disease? An opportunity to heal. Hatred? An opportunity to love. Temptation? An opportunity to overcome. Sin? An opportunity to forgive. Jesus turned trials into triumphs. — John C. Maxwell, *How High Will You Climb? Determine Your*

Success by Cultivating the Right Attitude (Nashville: Thomas Nelson, 2014).

9. Doesn't this passage seem impossible? How can we ever live it?

The Sermon on the Mount isn't just about us. If it was, we might admire it as a fine bit of idealism, but we'd then return to our normal lives. It's about Jesus himself. This was the blueprint for his own life. He asks nothing of his followers that he hasn't faced himself. And, within his own life, we can already sense a theme that will grow larger and larger until we can't miss it. If this is the way to show what God is really like, and if this is the pattern that Jesus himself followed exactly, Matthew is inviting us to draw the conclusion: that in Jesus we see the Emmanuel, the God-with-us person. The Sermon on the Mount isn't just about how to behave. It's about discovering the living God in the loving, and dying, Jesus, and learning to reflect that love ourselves into the world that needs it so badly. — Tom Wright, *Matthew for Everyone, Part 1: Chapters 1-15* (London: Society for Promoting Christian Knowledge, 2004), 53.

10. Verse 44. How does praying for our enemies change us?

I'll tell you a secret: If you pray for your enemies—for the people who bug you the most—you will experience power in your life and an ability to love them that will blow you away. Why? When you pray for your enemies, two things happen: They change and you change. It might take some time, but slowly yet surely, you'll see a change. If I'm praying every day for the guy I can't stand, something amazing happens. I become involved with him and interested in him. As I pray for him, there is a linkage established through prayer. — Jon Courson, *Jon Courson's Application Commentary* (Nashville, TN: Thomas Nelson, 2003), 30.

11. How does loving and praying for our enemies change them? Does anyone have a story?

Geo was quietly rejoicing as he fervently preached the gospel of Christ to the group sitting in front of him. The 40-year-old man could not resist thinking back 25 years earlier when he was in this exact spot.

In those days, he accompanied his grandfather and uncle as they traveled up and down the river, preaching the gospel. Their goal was to tell the story of Jesus in every village, but they were rejected and driven out of each one.

He remembered this village of the Saramaccan (sair-ah-MAH-can) people group. His grandfather had led the village medium to Christ. The respected medium destroyed his fetishes and materials used in magic rituals. The villagers became so furious, however, that they threw rocks at young Geo and his relatives.

The three jumped into their boat and were able to make it safely back home. Later that same night, however, those offended villagers raided Geo's village. All the villagers were pulled from their huts. When the men found Geo's grandfather, they brought him out, whipped him with a chain from a chainsaw and poured tar over his gaping wounds. Geo ran and hid in the jungle to watch.

Now it was 25 years later, and Geo was back in the same village where he had been rejected. During the years, God worked in Geo's heart to forgive that village. He reminded them of the event 25 years ago and extended an invitation to follow Christ. That night, 30 Sara-maccans trusted Jesus as Savior. —TIM AND JUDY, MIDDLE AMERICA AND THE CARIBBEAN / Beth Moore, *Voices of the Faithful: Inspiring Stories of Courage from Christians Serving around the World* (Nashville: Thomas Nelson, 2005).

12. Who are our enemies? Who is an example of someone you might consider an enemy?

WHEN MY LITTLE SISTER, LISA, WAS BORN ON MY THIRD birthday, my parents told me that she was my birthday present from God. We've been inseparable ever since. Of course we endured occasional sibling rivalries and conflicts, but she was always my baby sis, whom I loved as much as anyone else in the world. She still is.

I always believed I was her protector. Like a mother lion protecting her cubs, I was the big brother looking out for his little sis. Truthfully, there were times I enjoyed my protective role a bit too much—like the time I conveniently sat on the front porch cleaning my shotgun when her boyfriend came to pick her up. For some reason, that guy didn't stick around very long.

You can imagine how I felt when I learned of the tragedy. I found out that my little sister had been molested for years by a close family friend. Max had been Lisa's sixth-grade teacher. He taught me to play racquetball, shopped at my dad's retail store, and often cheered for my sister at her school drill-team performances. At the time, this single man in his midthirties seemed like a nice person looking for friends. Our family readily accepted him, unaware that behind the supportive teacher facade was a very sick man who repeatedly abused numerous girls over many years.

To say that I wanted Max to die and burn in hell doesn't even begin to convey how much I wanted him to suffer. Although the words rage, hate, and revenge come to mind when I think about Max, the English language simply doesn't have a word for what I felt. — Craig Groeschel, *The Christian Atheist: When You Believe in God but Live as If He Doesn't Exist* (Grand Rapids, MI: Zondervan, 2010).

13. This may seem a little simplistic, but… what is an enemy? How would you define it?

Now the word "enemies" sounds like kind of an extreme term, and some of you may be thinking, I don't have any enemies. But you do, because an enemy is anybody you find hard to love. Sometimes it's the person sitting next to you. Jesus said to love them, your enemies. Do you do that? It's very hard to trust Jesus with this command of his. Something inside us says, This is not natural! They don't deserve it. If I love them, how do I know they're going to get what's coming to them?

Maybe your enemy is someone who has done something really bad. Maybe they've lied about you, cheated you, betrayed you, abused you, smeared your reputation, taken money from you, squelched you, or belittled you. Jesus says to love them. Jesus loved the people who killed him. He knows about enemies. — John Ortberg, *Now What? God's Guide to Life for Graduates* (Grand Rapids, MI: Zondervan, 2011).

14. How does God feel about our enemies?

Today, take a lesson from Oswald Chambers. Those people who pass you on the street, who ride with you in the elevator, who stand ahead of you in the grocery checkout line—every one of them is unique. Every one of them has been carefully designed by God and is loved by God. Pray today for those with whom you come in contact. Look past the circumstances that brought them you way and see them as the wonderful "human stuff" that Chambers speaks of. Never lump people into stereotypical groups. In God's eyes, there are no stereotypes—only his magnificent creations. — Nick Harrison, *Magnificent Prayer: 366 Devotions to Deepen Your Prayer Experience* (Grand Rapids, MI: Zondervan, 2010).

15. Have you ever prayed for an enemy? Who has a story?

As I sat in church one Sunday, my pastor preached a convicting message on forgiveness, explaining how we should release those who've wronged us. As he read the words from Scripture commanding me to forgive, everything in me screamed, No! I don't want to forgive Max! I refuse to release him!

My pastor preached on. And God ever-so-slowly chipped away at the rough edges of my heart. As church neared its end, I walked alone to the altar to ask God for his help to forgive. I remember telling God that I knew I should forgive this man I hated, but I didn't want to. And even if I did want to, I wouldn't know how to forgive such a wrong.

The next week, in my personal Bible study, I came across a verse that helped to soften my heart a bit more. In Luke 6:28, Jesus teaches us to "bless those who curse you, pray for those who mistreat you." I'm supposed to pray for those who mistreat me? Sure, I'll pray for Max. I'll ask God to give him a case of eternal hemorrhoids. I certainly wasn't ready to pray for anything good.

Later I stumbled across another one of Jesus' annoying commands. This one is found in Matthew 5:43 – 44, where Jesus says, "You have heard that it was said, 'Love your neighbor and hate your enemy.' But I tell you: Love your enemies and pray for those who persecute you." There it was again—love and pray for your enemies!

Knowing I couldn't ignore this command any longer, I tried to pray for Max. In all honesty, I didn't pray that God would bless him in every way. I didn't ask that God would shower his love upon Max with a godly wife, healthy children, and a long and prosperous life. At the same time, I didn't ask God to torture him eternally in hell. In sheer obedience to God, I simply prayed a grudging but obedient three-second prayer: "God, I pray you work in his life."

Over the weeks and months, I continued uttering those same words. At first it was as painful as walking barefoot on burning coals. But eventually it became more bearable. Then I actually started to mean what I was praying. God, work in his life.

When we're told to pray for those who've hurt us, I'm convinced our prayers are as much for ourselves as they are for the offender. As God has helped me move beyond my Christian Atheist doubts about prayer, now I see an added value of praying for those who hurt me. My prayers for others may or may not change them. But my prayers always change me.

Praying for Max over time changed me. It made me a different person, so different that I began to contemplate the impossible: asking God to help me forgive Max. — Craig Groeschel, *The Christian Atheist: When You Believe in God but Live as If He Doesn't Exist* (Grand Rapids, MI: Zondervan, 2010).

16. How? How do we love our enemies? How do we love people who are hard to love?

The idea in Galatians is that the faith that unites you to Christ spontaneously leads to love. Often, methods of following Christ are taught that come with a bunch of new laws to follow—it almost becomes a new Mount Sinai. It's a great mercy to meditate on a passage like Galatians 5:13—6:10. The Holy Spirit will use these verses to show you how your life can be a life of love; he can give you the confidence to believe that you already have this love through faith.

Once you are convinced of these things, you can do almost anything. But if you aren't convinced of the power and wonder of Jesus's love for you, of your free justification and that you are God's dearly loved son or daughter, and that his love is unconditional, it's very hard to love others. Faith leads to love. It doesn't matter how weak you are, how many sins you've committed, or what kind of self-image you have. Following Christ is about serving others in love, and we have the power do it because Christ is in us. That's how he lived his life, and it's how he's empowering us to live ours. — C. John Miller and Rose Marie Miller, *Saving Grace: Daily Devotions from Jack Miller* (Greensboro, NC: New Growth Press, 2014).

17. Why doesn't God just make all our enemies go away?

In fact, if God wants to grow some quality in you, he may send you a person who tempts you to behave in just the opposite way. If you need to develop love, then some unlovable people will be your greatest challenge. If you need to develop hope, maintaining it in the face of discouragers will make it strong. If you want to grow in your ability to confront, a hard-to-confront intimidator will give you serious practice. As lifting weights strengthens a muscle and cardio exercises strengthen a heart, difficult people can strengthen our ability to love.

Why does God allow difficult people in my life?

What other kind are there?

If God were to get rid of all the difficult people in the world — if he were to remove everybody with quirks, flaws, ugliness, and sin — you would get awfully lonely.

We always wish that God would give us a life without difficult people in it. But how many great characters in the Bible had difficult people in their lives? Moses had Pharaoh, Elijah had Jezebel, Esther had Haman, Jacob had Laban, David had Saul, John the Baptist had Herod. Even Jesus had Judas. If God loves you and wants to shape you, he will send some difficult people your way. But take heart. You are the difficult person he is sending to shape somebody else!

If we can learn to have rivers of living water still flowing through us in these relationships, we will be unstoppable. — John Ortberg, *The Me I Want to Be* (Grand Rapids, MI: Zondervan, 2010).

18. Verse 45. What does the sunrise teach us—or remind us—about what it means to be godly?

In Matthew 5:45, Jesus speaks of God's fairness and graciousness. Every morning the sun gives another day's life to all humanity, whether evil or good. Refreshing showers fall on the lawns of committed Christians and of their pagan neighbors. While some blessings are reserved only for the children of God, others are common to the entire world.

In the same way, some burdens are borne by believers, such as persecution or sorrow over lost souls. But other burdens are shared by all humanity, and being a Christian doesn't make us immune from trials. Even seasoned Christians need to remember this, or else we'll find ourselves thinking, If God loves me so, why am I in such painful straits? Why don't other people have these problems?

Sorrow is universal, but for the believer, it is redemptive, because God turns it to good. Dr. F. B. Meyer wrote, "In suffering and sorrow God touches the minor chords, develops the passive virtues, and opens to view the treasures of darkness, the constellations of promise, the rainbow of hope, the silver light of the covenant."

Trust Him today, and rejoice in His mercies whether it's sunny or raining. — David Jeremiah, *Turning Points with God: 365 Daily Devotions* (Carol Stream, IL: Tyndale, 2014).

19. How does God's love for us and others make us more loving?

God loves you simply because he has chosen to do so.

He loves you when you don't feel lovely.

He loves you when no one else loves you. Others may abandon you, divorce you, and ignore you, but God will love you. Always. No matter what.

This is his sentiment: "I'll call nobodies and make them somebodies; I'll call the unloved and make them beloved" (Rom. 9:25 MSG).

This is his promise. "I have loved you, my people, with an everlasting love. With unfailing love I have drawn you to myself" (Jer. 31:3 NLT).

Do you know what else that means? You have a deep aquifer of love from which to draw. When you find it hard to love, then you need a drink! Drink deeply! Drink daily! — *A Love Worth Giving* / Max Lucado, *Grace for the Moment® Volume Ii: More Inspirational Thoughts for Each Day of the Year* (Nashville: Thomas Nelson, 2006).

20. Let's close in prayer. I want to invite you to articulate a prayer in response to the passages we have been studying.

Lord, I have heard that it was said, "Love your neighbor and hate your enemy." But You tell me to love my enemies and pray for those who persecute me, that I might be a child of my Father in heaven (Matt. 5:43-44).

Father God, if I love those who love me, what reward will I get? Are not even the godless doing that? And if I greet only those to whom I am close, what am I doing more than others? Do not even pagans do that? (Matt. 5:46-47).

You have called me to be different, Lord! You have called me to go far beyond the actions of even the noblest pagan. Help me not to be overcome by evil but to overcome evil with good (Rom. 12:21). — Beth Moore, *Praying God's Word Day by Day* (Nashville: B&H, 2006).

Matthew 7.13 – 27

OPEN

Let's each share your name and where you live.

DIG

1. Matthew 7.13, 14. Someone take a stab at paraphrasing this passage.

Although I wanted to believe I was one of the few, my heart knew I was stuck in a traffic jam. Jesus' words screamed like a big neon sign, pointing out a route that I had failed to notice as I tried to keep up with the convoy of normalcy. The truth of his words suddenly seemed so clear.

The majority of people — the crowd — is traveling the wrong path, the one that leads to destruction. They're the normal ones — intent on looking like the rest, spending money like the rest, living like the rest, keeping up with the rest. But their road leads to a dead end. Only a few people — the weird ones unafraid to exit the normal highway — find the right road. Not many, but a small and brave group of travelers willing to separate from the crowd and embark on a different kind of journey down a less obvious path.

Talk about a major U-turn! Here I was, comfortably cruising down the interstate at eighty miles per hour, assuming I was headed in the right direction since everyone else was going the same way, when suddenly the GPS revealed that where I really wanted to go was in the opposite direction on a small back road. To really follow Jesus, to know him, meant that I'd have to be different from my friends and everyone else. But I didn't want to be different, one of those goofy Christians I'd seen around campus with their guitars and clever little tracts that weren't supposed to look like tracts. Christians were different and different was weird and I was committed to being normal.

And since I didn't want to be weird, I wasn't about to change my course and follow Jesus. — Craig Groeschel, *Weird: Because Normal Isn't Working* (Grand Rapids, MI: Zondervan, 2011).

2. In this classic passage, Jesus describes two paths. What is the broad path like?

MANY OF US have been looking for Easy Street all of our lives. But what happens when we get on Easy Street?

Bits and Pieces, a fascinating little magazine, gives us the answer in the form of some Hawaiian wisdom from the island of Oahu. If you take the Pali Highway northbound out of Honolulu, you will come to Pali Pass. At Pali Pass you can turn right on Park Street, go one block, and you will arrive at Easy Street. Turn left on Easy Street and drive one block; you will then see a sign that reads "Dead End."

> I have sometimes seen more in a line of the Bible than I could well tell how to stand under, and yet at another time the whole Bible hath been to me as dry as a stick.
> —JOHN BUNYAN

The article concluded, "Those looking for the easy street of life are usually surprised by the road's predictable destination." To this, I would add that life has its ups and downs, and it really is tough. However, when we are tough on ourselves, life is infinitely easier on us. In short, everything is not going to be easy. Many things are going to be difficult, but we arrive on a much easier street by overcoming difficulties.

As a salesman and as a sales trainer, I frequently have made the observation that the toughies are the teachers. When we encounter a prospect ready to buy, it's fun to write the order, but we don't learn anything from the transaction. When we meet a legitimate prospect who has lots of objections and gives us many reasons why he should not buy, and we effectively deal with him, we learn something about how to make other sales, which brings us even more success.

We read in Matthew 7:13-14 (NLT): "You can enter God's Kingdom only through the narrow gate. The highway to hell is broad, and its gate is wide for the many who choose the easy way. But the gateway to life is small, and the road is narrow, and only a few ever find it." The good news is that for those who do find it, God's promises are magnificent. — Zig Ziglar, *Staying Up, Up, up in a Down, down World: Daily Hope for the Daily Grind* (Nashville: Thomas Nelson, 2000).

3. Why is it that only a few find the path that leads to life?

As I dived into my new passion for Bible study, I noticed that certain words were printed in red and not black—the words of Jesus. As if what he was saying didn't stand out enough! When I read what Jesus taught, it was anything but normal. His teachings were so weird that they could easily be considered otherworldly.

Jesus said, "Love your enemies, do good to those who hate you, bless those who curse you, pray for those who mistreat you. If someone strikes you on one cheek, turn to him the other also" (Luke 6:27 – 29).

Normal says to hate your enemies. Jesus says to love them.

Normal seeks revenge on those who hurt you. Jesus shows you how to be kind to those who harm you.

If someone hits you, then normal swings back. Jesus teaches you to turn the other cheek.

Let's be honest. This is not only counterintuitive to everything we learned on the playground in elementary school; it's just downright weird. And these are not the most challenging of his unusual teachings. Jesus also told us to pray for those who persecute us. Weird. And if we want to find our lives, we have to lose them. Weirder. And if we don't hate our parents, we really aren't committed to him. Weirdest. — Craig Groeschel, *Weird: Because Normal Isn't Working* (Grand Rapids, MI: Zondervan, 2011).

4. How many Christians would you say are on the narrow path?

Although I had always believed in God, I had to acknowledge that I didn't really know him or what it meant to follow him. Maybe the weird I associated with religious people wasn't how he intended Christians to be different. Maybe there was a whole new wild world of weird that came with choosing the narrow path. Maybe it was time to abandon the normal and wide path I'd known and off-road it for a wonderful weirdness I couldn't imagine. — Craig Groeschel, *Weird: Because Normal Isn't Working* (Grand Rapids, MI: Zondervan, 2011).

5. We always want to read the Bible for application. What is the application of this passage for our day-to-day lives?

After a Tuesday night Bible meeting, I walked alone to an empty soft-ball field. No matter what it cost me — even being normal — I had decided that I wanted to know Jesus and live for him. I wanted to do life his way and not mine. As I knelt beside the dugout and prayed, I left normal behind and embraced whatever it took—being different to the point of the God kind of weird — to follow Jesus. Something melted within me, and I walked away forever changed, with a sense of God's grace I can't describe.

It didn't take long for others to notice the change. When I told my fraternity brothers and teammates that I'd become a Christian, they gazed at me with the tentative uncertainty usually reserved for wild animals and mental patients. They quickly realized, however, that I wasn't dangerous—just weird. In a matter of moments, I'd gone from a cool, normal, somewhat popular, regular kind of guy to a first-class Jesus freak.

Perhaps the most immediately noticeable change was my commitment to purity — no more sex until marriage. To say the least, my sex-obsessed buddies thought I had really lost it and had drunk more than my share of the bad Kool-Aid. Several frat guys even wagered a hundred dollars that I wouldn't last one month without going back to my old ways. For the record, they lost their money! — Craig Groeschel, *Weird: Because Normal Isn't Working* (Grand Rapids, MI: Zondervan, 2011).

6. How is the narrow way better than the broad path? Be specific.

However, nowadays being normal isn't quite as easy and painless as it once seemed to be. In fact, it's more time consuming than ever. There aren't enough hours in the day to buy, sell, drive, cook, clean, call, shop, eat, plan, study, write, review, schedule, and follow through on everything. Overwhelmed, overloaded, and exhausted, everybody talks about wanting more time, but only to "catch up" on what they're already doing — rushing, planning, worrying, and rushing some more. Families suffer. Health wanes. Priorities fade. Joy evaporates. Most people don't know their life's direction because their soul is dizzy from spinning around so much. Uninterrupted time to rest, relax, and enjoy life sounds like a line from a retirement home brochure. Normal is busy and getting busier.

When it comes to finances, it's normal to go into debt so deep that you can't see the way out. Money becomes a dark pit of worry, fear, anxiety, tension, and fighting. Most people I know are living paycheck to paycheck. Most make more money today than they ever have, but it's never enough. Now more than ever, it's expensive to be normal — so much cool stuff to buy and take care of, so many normal experiences you want your family to have. Only it's hard to enjoy any of it when the financial noose tightens with each monthly payment.

Normal relationships require little and provide less. You and your spouse are so busy, so stressed, and so exhausted, there's normally no time for each other. No wonder, then, that affairs are the norm. They provide the attention, romance, and sex without the commitment, sacrifice, or intimacy required in marriage. Similarly, you'd love to spend more time with the kids, but there's just not enough time. They're almost as busy and stressed as you are. It would be great to have deep, meaningful conversations and shared experiences that allow you to teach them what you know. Normal families, however, just don't work that way.

And nothing's more normal than sex, right? Premarital sex, extramarital sex, friends-with-benefits type sex. Porn, experimentation, casual hookups — whatever feels good between consenting adults. It's totally normal. Maybe our parents were uptight and repressed about sex, but we're more progressive, more liberated nowadays. In the twenty-first century, why in the world would anyone remain a virgin until marriage? After all, as one of my frat brothers used to say, "You wouldn't buy the car without test driving it first, would you?" Unfortunately, though, normal also carries a hefty price: guilt, shame, confusion, remorse, disease, addiction, unwanted children, and divorce.

Normal infects our faith as well, both what we believe and how we live it out. When we consider how people relate to God, it's normal to either reject God altogether or believe in him while living as if he doesn't exist. In churches, normal is lukewarm Christianity, self-centered spiritual consumerism, and shallow, me-driven faith. God has become a means to an end, a tool in our toolbox to accomplish what we want. The majority of people claim to know God, but by their actions they deny him.

And all this is normal. — Craig Groeschel, *Weird: Because Normal Isn't Working* (Grand Rapids, MI: Zondervan, 2011).

7. **Do you think the people on the narrow path feel a little bit like weirdos?**

In this book, I'm going to challenge you to jump off the normal path and onto one that may seem a little weird. At times, you're going to argue, "But, Craig — that's just too weird!" When that happens, we're likely making progress. We're going to talk about dramatic changes. Because, let's face it, if small changes would've made the difference, you'd have made those changes a long time ago. Everyone travels along the wide road; only a few take the narrow path. — Craig Groeschel, *Weird: Because Normal Isn't Working* (Grand Rapids, MI: Zondervan, 2011).

8. **What price do those pay who stay on the broad path? Again, give specific examples.**

Instead of living stressed, overwhelmed, and exhausted, you can live a life of meaningful relationships, intentional scheduling, and deep, fulfilling rest for your soul. Instead of choking with constant financial fear and tension, you can let God's Word lead you along a path to financial peace, margin, and eternal investments. Instead of allowing your marriage to drift into parallel lives or divorce by default, you can experience true intimacy with your spouse. Rather than continuing on the normal sexual path toward pain, emptiness, and idolatry, you can allow God to heal you, change the way you think, and place deliberate safeguards in your life to protect you. God wants you to know him and love him — not just acknowledge him or consider him a cosmic sugar daddy.

If you let him, if you choose not to coast along the world's wide-open road but rather to blaze a narrow trail with Jesus as your guide, then you'll never settle for normal again. You'll want only one thing.

The God kind of weird. — Craig Groeschel, *Weird: Because Normal Isn't Working* (Grand Rapids, MI: Zondervan, 2011).

9. Matthew 7.15. What false prophets should we watch out for today? Name names.

In Jude's brief letter to believers, the apostle firmly warns against false prophets and tells us how to respond to them. "Keep yourselves in the love of God" (Jude 21). Our primary response to false teaching is simply to be right with God in the first place, to make sure we are in fellowship with Him and receiving His blessing and power. Then we can "have mercy on some, who are doubting" (v. 22, NASB)—believers who doubt their faith because of false teachers need reassurance.

Another necessary response might be to "save others, snatching them out of the fire" (v. 23, NASB)—unbelievers bound for hell after hearing false teaching need to be rescued before it's too late.

Finally, Jude tells about a third response to false prophets: "On some have mercy with fear, hating even the garment polluted by the flesh" (v. 23, NASB). We sometimes must confront false prophets and their followers, doing so with a special dependence on the Lord and being careful not to get contaminated by their false teachings. — John MacArthur, *Truth for Today : A Daily Touch of God's Grace* (Nashville, Tenn.: J. Countryman, 2001), 250.

10. Do a search on your phone for the phrase, "false prophets today." Read over the list. Do you agree with the list?

The Didache, one of the earliest Christian writings after the New Testament, gives several guidelines for discerning true from false prophets. First, a true prophet will not wear out his welcome but will move on, tending to his ministry and mission. But a false prophet may hang around indefinitely, concerned only about serving his own interests.

Second, unlike the false prophet, the true prophet is averse to excessive appeals for money. He is content with support for the basic needs of life and ministry.

Third, a true prophet's lifestyle will correspond to the righteous standards he teaches. A false prophet very likely will teach one thing and practice another.

A true minister of the gospel will demonstrate what Paul wrote, "For we are not, as so many, peddling the word of God; but as of sincerity, but as from God, we speak in the sight of God in Christ" (2 Cor. 2:17). — John MacArthur, Truth for Today : A Daily Touch of God's Grace (Nashville, Tenn.: J. Countryman, 2001), 251.

11. What harm comes from not recognizing a false prophet?

The most dangerous characteristic of false prophets is that they claim to be from God and to speak for Him. "The prophets prophesy falsely, and the priests rule by their own power; and My people love to have it so" (Jer. 5:31).

Such leaders nearly always appear pleasant and positive. They like to be with Christians, and they know how to talk and act like believers.

False prophets usually exude sincerity and thereby more easily deceive others (see 2 Tim. 3:13). But you can identify false teachers' true colors by noting what they do not talk much about. They usually don't deny basic doctrines such as Christ's deity and substitutionary atonement, the sinfulness of humanity, or unbelievers' going to hell. They simply ignore such "controversial" truths.

But whenever a false prophet is in your midst, you must not ignore his presence or the harmful effects of his heretical teaching. — John MacArthur, Truth for Today : A Daily Touch of God's Grace (Nashville, Tenn.: J. Countryman, 2001), 249.

12. What harm comes from confusing a true prophet with a false prophet?

I think there are some who think it is spiritual to discover the secret flaws of some famous preachers. I have had people walk out on my teaching because I said something nice about

Bill Hybels or Rick Warren. I don't agree with everything these two men teach. In fact, I doubt I agree with everything anyone preaches! But I have listened to many sermons by both of them and for the life of my I don't understand the accusations of heresy for either of them.

13. What makes a false prophet a false prophet? We disagree on many things—predestination vss. free will, speaking in tongues, women in ministry, and so on. What are things we can have a friendly disagreement on, and what are things that make someone outside the tent of orthodoxy?

There are a number of doctrinal characteristics of cults. One will typically find an emphasis on new revelation from God, a denial of the sole authority of the Bible, a denial of the Trinity, a distorted view of God and Jesus, or a denial of salvation by grace.

New Revelation. Many cult leaders claim to have a direct pipeline to God. The teachings of the cult often change and, hence, they need new "revelations" to justify such changes. Mormons, for example, once excluded African Americans from the priesthood. When social pressure was exerted against the Mormon church for this blatant form of racism, the Mormon president received a new "revelation" reversing the previous decree. Jehovah's Witnesses engaged in the same kind of change regarding the earlier Watchtower teaching that vaccinations and organ transplants were prohibited by Jehovah.

Denial of the Sole Authority of the Bible. Many cults deny the sole authority of the Bible. The Mormons, for example, believe the Book of Mormon is higher Scripture than the Bible. Jim Jones, founder and leader of Jonestown, placed himself in authority over the Bible. Christian Scientists elevate Mary Baker Eddy's book Science and Health to supreme authority. Reverend Moon placed his book The Divine Principle in authority over all his followers. New Agers believe in many modern forms of authoritative revelation, such as The Aquarian Gospel of Jesus the Christ.

A Distorted View of God and Jesus. Many cults set forth a distorted view of God and Jesus. The "Jesus Only" Oneness Pentecostals, for example, deny the Trinity and hold to a form of modalism, claiming that Jesus is God, and that "Father," "Son," and "Holy Spirit" are simply singular names for Jesus. The Jehovah's Witnesses deny both the Trinity and the absolute deity of Christ, saying that Christ is a lesser god than the Father (who is God Almighty). The Mormons say Jesus was "procreated" (by a heavenly father and a heavenly mother) at a point in time, and was the spirit–brother of Lucifer. Mormons do speak of a "Trinity," but redefine it into Tritheism (i.e., three gods). The Baha'is say Jesus was just one of many prophets of God. The Jesus of the spiritists is just an advanced medium. The Jesus of the Theosophists is a mere reincarnation of the so–called World Teacher (who is said to periodically reincarnate in the body of a human disciple). The Jesus of psychic Edgar Cayce is a being who in his first incarnation was Adam and in his thirtieth reincarnation was "the Christ."

Related to the above, cults also typically deny the bodily resurrection of Jesus Christ. The Jehovah's Witnesses, for example, say that Jesus was raised from the dead as an invisible spirit creature. Herbert W. Armstrong, founder of the Worldwide Church of God, also denied the physical, bodily resurrection of Christ. (Note that in recent years the Worldwide Church of God has repudiated many of Armstrong's teachings and has taken significant steps toward orthodoxy.)

Denial of Salvation by Grace. Cults typically deny salvation by grace, thus distorting the purity of the gospel. The Mormons, for example, emphasize the necessity of becoming more and more perfect in this life. The Jehovah's Witnesses emphasize the importance of distributing Watchtower literature door–to–door as a part of "working out" their salvation. Herbert W. Armstrong said that the idea that works are not required for salvation is rooted in Satan.

From the brief survey above, it is clear that all cults deny one or more of the fundamental, essential doctrines of Christianity. — Norman L. Geisler and Ron Rhodes, *When*

Cultists Ask: A Popular Handbook on Cultic Misinterpretations (Grand Rapids, MI: Baker Books, 1997).

14. Matthew 7.21 – 23. What do we learn about who goes to Heaven and who doesn't from this passage?

Have you ever heard of George Brett, the legendary third baseman who played for the Kansas City Royals? When I was a kid, I collected every George Brett baseball card ever made and knew everything about his career.

In 1988, I played in the NAIA National Tennis Championship in Kansas City. On a walk downtown, I saw George Brett sitting at an outdoor cafe. I couldn't stop myself—I walked right up to him, extended my hand, and said, "I know this happens to you all the time. I'm so sorry. I just had to tell you, you're the man! In 1980, you batted .390—you almost batted over .400—which would have broken Ted Williams' record from back in 1941. You had 118 RBIs in only 117 games. You're the man!" (A bit repetitive, I know, but I was nervous.)

Now, I didn't actually know George Brett, but I knew information about him. And I had heard that he was cocky and rude. What I experienced, however, was quite the opposite.

"You know all that about me?" he asked.

"Oh, I'm just getting started."

"That's amazing. Why don't you sit with us? Let's talk for a few minutes." And he pulled up a chair.

After we had talked for about fifteen minutes, George asked, "So, what brings you to Kansas City?" I told him that I was playing in the big tennis tournament the next day. He congratulated me and said, "You know what? You've watched me all these years. I'll try to come out and watch you play tomorrow."

The next day, I won the National Tennis title...with George Brett cheering me on from the very front row. (Cue dream scene fade-out and ethereal musical sounds.)

Okay, so that didn't really happen, though it would have been a great ending to this story. The reality is that George didn't show, and I lost in the second round and went home crushed.

Technically, I could say that I know George Brett because of our single encounter. But it's obvious I don't really know him. If you were to remind him about our encounter in Kansas City, he might not remember at all.

Now let's rewind the history tape a couple thousand years. When the apostle Paul wrote his letter to the Galatians (Jesus-followers who lived in the region of Galatia, modern-day Turkey), they had experienced the real, living God but had recently become trapped in legalism. They knew God, but not well enough to avoid getting sucked back into a life based in the law, rather than in love. In Galatians 4:8 – 9, Paul wrote, "Formerly, when you did not know God, you were slaves to those who by nature are not gods. But now that you know God—or rather are known by God—how is it that you are turning back to those weak and miserable principles? Do you wish to be enslaved by them all over again?"

Paul essentially was saying, "You know God, but not well enough to avoid your old habits—the attitudes that hurt you and your closeness to God." In the twenty-first century, we would be wise to ask ourselves, "Is this us too?"

Maybe we "sort of" know God. Maybe sometime in the past we've prayed and asked Jesus to transform our lives. Maybe we have a basic understanding of God. Maybe, once, we genuinely felt close to him. But we don't know him well now.
— Craig Groeschel, *The Christian Atheist: When You Believe in God but Live as If He Doesn't Exist* (Grand Rapids, MI: Zondervan, 2010).

15. What exactly does it mean to know Jesus?

Finally, there are those people who know God intimately and serve him with their whole hearts. For me, I know this is happening when I'm becoming increasingly aware of God's presence within me, his provision, his power, and his peace. I don't feel like God's "out there," waiting for me to direct a prayer his way every now and then. It's more like an ongoing conversation: "Hi, God. Hey listen, what do you think of this?" Then I honestly believe God speaks to me through his written Word and by his Spirit.

It's like somehow my spirit is connected to him, and I can hear what he's saying. There's kind of a buzz, a constant conscious awareness that as my day unfolds, God is orchestrating things and sending people into my life. That's doing life with God.

At other times, God may not feel as close. But by faith, I know he is with me. No matter what I feel, I hold the assurance that God never leaves me. And he won't leave you.

The psalmist David describes in Psalm 63:1 – 4 his relationship with God. In fact, he says that his experience of knowing the personal God creates a deeper longing for even more intimate knowledge of God. Verse 1 begins, "O God, you are my God." You're not somebody else's God, that I've just heard about. You're my God. — Craig Groeschel, *The Christian Atheist: When You Believe in God but Live as If He Doesn't Exist* (Grand Rapids, MI: Zondervan, 2010).

16. Isn't there a magic prayer we can pray to insure us a place in Heaven?

One Friday night during my ninth grade year, however, my Sunday school teacher told us that according to Matthew 7:21–23 many people who think they know Jesus will awaken on that final day to the reality that He never really knew them. Though they had prayed a prayer to receive Jesus, they had never really been born again and never taken the lordship of Jesus seriously. They would, my teacher explained, be turned away from heaven into everlasting punishment with the disastrous words, "I never knew you; depart from Me, you who practice lawlessness!"

I was terrified. Would I be one of those ones turned away? Had I really been "sorry" for my sins at age five? And could I really have known what I was doing at age four?

So I asked Jesus to come into my heart again, this time with a resolve to be much more intentional about my faith. I requested re-baptism, and gave a very moving testimony in front of our congregation about getting serious with God.

Case closed, right? Wrong.

Not long after that I found myself asking again: Had I really been sorry enough for my sin this time around? I'd see some people weep rivers of tears when they got saved, but I hadn't. Did that mean I was not really sorry? And there were a few sins I seemed to fall back into over and over again, no matter how many resolutions I made to do better. Was I really sorry for those sins? Was that prayer a moment of total surrender? Would I have died for Jesus at that moment if He'd asked?

So I prayed the sinner's prayer again. And again. And again. Each time trying to get it right, each time really trying to mean it. I would have a moment when I felt like I got it right, followed by a temporary euphoria. But it would fade quickly and I'd question it all again. And so I'd pray again.

I walked a lot of aisles during those days. I think I've been saved at least once in every denomination.

Because I understood baptism to be a post-salvation confession of faith, each time I gained a little assurance, I felt like I should get re-baptized. Four times, total. Honestly, it got pretty embarrassing. I became a staple at our church's baptism services. I got my own locker in the baptismal changing area.

It was a wretched experience. My spiritual life was characterized by cycles of doubt, aisle-walking, and submersion in water. I could not find the assurance of salvation no matter how often, or how sincerely, I asked Jesus into my heart.

I used to think I was alone in this struggle, but as I've shared my story over the years so many have come forward to tell me that my experience was theirs (usually minus the baptisms and the OCD tendencies) that I've concluded this problem is epidemic in the church. — J. D. Greear, *Stop Asking Jesus into Your Heart* (Nashville: B&H, 2013).

17. Is it possible to think you are Heaven-bound when you are not?

This is a very serious question, not just because it keeps some people in a state of fear, but because others are getting it dead wrong.

Jesus warned that there are a vast number of people who seem assured of a salvation they don't actually possess. My Sunday school teacher was telling us the truth: according to Matthew 7, Jesus will turn away "many" on that last day who thought they belonged to Him. There's no doubt that many of those will have prayed a sinner's prayer.

One afternoon I was at a local basketball court and started a pickup game with a guy I'd seen there a few times. He was quite a character—he cursed like a sailor and had so many tattoos on his body I wasn't sure what the actual color of his skin was. He boasted continually about how many girls he was sleeping with. He wasn't the kind of guy you'd suspect knew his way around the Bible.

As we played our game, I began to share my story of how I came to Christ. About three sentences into it, he stopped, grabbed the ball, and said, "Dude, are you trying to witness to me?"

Surprised he even knew the term witness, I said, "Uhhh . . . well . . . yes."

He said, "That's awesome. No one has tried to witness to me in a long time. . . . But don't worry about me. I went to youth camp when I was thirteen and I asked Jesus to come into my heart. And I was legit. I became a super-Christian. I went to youth group every week, I did the "true love waits" commitment thing, I memorized verses, and I went on mission trips. I even led other friends to Jesus.

"About two years after that, however, I 'discovered' sex. And I didn't like the idea of a god telling me who I could have sex with. So I decided to put God on hold for a while, and after a while just quit believing in Him altogether. I'm a happy atheist now."

He then added: "But here's what's awesome: the church I grew up in was Southern Baptist, and they taught eternal security—that means 'once saved, always saved.' By the way, aren't you a Baptist?" — J. D. Greear, *Stop Asking Jesus into Your Heart* (Nashville: B&H, 2013).

18. How common do you suppose this is—to think you are Heaven-bound and you are not?

In His parable about the different types of soil, Jesus spoke of a group who heard His word and made an initial, encouraging response of belief, only to fade away over time. These are those, Jesus explained, who hear the gospel and respond positively to it—i.e., pray the prayer, walk the aisle, get baptized, or do whatever new converts in your church do. They remain in the church for a period of time. But they do not endure when the sun of persecution comes out and will not in the end be saved (Luke 8:13).

The apostle John described a large group of people who "believed in His name" but to whom Jesus would not commit Himself because "He knew all men" (John 2:23–25). He knew their belief was a temporary fad that would not endure the test of time and trial.

These sobering stories teach us that many are headed into eternal judgment under the delusion of going to heaven. They were told that if they prayed the prayer, Jesus would save them, seal them, and never leave nor forsake them. They prayed that prayer and lived under the delusion they will go to heaven when they die. My blood runs cold just thinking about them.

A 2011 Barna study1 shows that nearly half of all adults in America have prayed such a prayer, and subsequently believe they are going to heaven, though many of them rarely, if ever, attend a church, read the Bible personally, or have lifestyles that differ in any significant way from those outside the church. If the groups described in Matthew 7 and Luke 8 are not referring to them, I don't know to whom they could be referring.

The Enemy—one of whose names in Scripture is "the Deceiver"—loves to keep truly saved believers unsure of their salvation because he knows that if he does they'll never experience the freedom, joy, and confidence that God wants them to have. But he also loves to keep those on their way to hell deluded into thinking they are on their way to heaven, their consciences immunized from Jesus' pleas to repent. — J. D. Greear, *Stop Asking Jesus into Your Heart* (Nashville: B&H, 2013).

19. How can anyone be sure they are Heaven-bound? How can anyone be sure they are not deceived?

He went on, "That means that my salvation at age thirteen still holds, even if I don't believe in God anymore now. 'Once saved, always saved,' right? That means that even if you're right, and God exists and Jesus is the only way, I'm safe! So either way, works out great for me. . . . If I'm right, then I haven't wasted my life curbing my lifestyle because of a fairy tale. OK, it's your shot."

What do you say to a person like that? Consider the facts: He had indeed prayed to ask Jesus into his heart, and all indications were that he was very sincere. And it's very possible for people to come to faith very early in life—Jesus, in fact, told adults to become like children if they want to be saved! Furthermore, this guy showed immediate "fruit" after his conversion, getting excited about Jesus and being busy for Him. And the Bible does indeed teach eternal security—once saved, always saved. So was he right? Can he, because he made a decision at some point in the past, live with the assurance that he is saved forever, regardless of how he lives now?

Here's the short answer, one I'll spend the rest of the book unpacking: he cannot. Salvation does indeed happen in a moment, and once you are saved you are always saved. The mark, however, of someone who is saved is that they maintain their confession of faith until the end of their lives. Salvation is not a prayer you pray in a one-time ceremony and then move on from; salvation is a posture of repentance and faith that you begin in a moment and maintain for the rest of your life. — J. D. Greear, *Stop Asking Jesus into Your Heart* (Nashville: B&H, 2013).

20. Suppose there was someone in the room who secretly doubted their salvation. What would you want to say to them? Imagine it is me. Imagine I doubt my salvation. What would you say to me? How would you help me?

Calling on sinners to seek salvation on the spot is not something invented by the Finney-Revivalist tradition. Throughout history, even some of the most Reformed evangelists have invited hearers to pray a sinner's prayer.

For example, Charles Spurgeon ended one of his sermons by saying,

> Before you leave this place, breathe an earnest prayer to God, saying, "God be merciful to me a sinner. Lord, I need to be saved. Save me. I call upon thy name." Join with me in prayer at this moment, I entreat you. Join with me while I put words into your mouths, and speak them on your behalf—"Lord, I am guilty. I deserve thy wrath. Lord, I cannot save myself. . . . I cast myself wholly upon thee, O Lord. I trust the blood and righteousness of thy dear Son; I trust thy mercy, and thy love, and thy power, as they are revealed in him. I dare to lay hold upon this word of thine, that whosoever shall call on the name of

the Lord shall be saved. Lord, save me tonight, for Jesus' sake. Amen."2

George Whitefield extended the same kind of invitations.3 John Bunyan described one of his characters, "Hopeful," being led through a sinner's prayer by another, "Faithful."4 The apostle Peter invited three thousand people to come forward for baptism in response to his first sermon (Acts 2:38). Ananias led Paul to call on God's name for forgiveness of sins after their first conversation (Acts 22:16).

So I am not, in any way, trying to discourage calling for a decision when we present the gospel. I am saying that above all else we must emphasize the absolute indispensability of repentance and faith for salvation. — J. D. Greear, *Stop Asking Jesus into Your Heart* (Nashville: B&H, 2013).

21. What do you want to recall from today's discussion?

22. How can we support one another in prayer this week?

Lesson #9, Matthew 8.5 – 13
Good Questions Have Groups Talking
www.joshhunt.com

Matthew 8.5 - 13

OPEN

Let's each share your name and one thing you are grateful for.

DIG

1. **In Matthew 8.5. We meet a centurion. What is a centurion?**

EVEN in the brief appearance that he makes on the stage of the New Testament story, this centurion is one of the most attractive characters in the gospels. The centurions were the backbone of the Roman army. In a Roman legion there were 6,000 men; the legion was divided into 60 centuries, each containing 100 men, and in command of each century there was a centurion. These centurions were the long-service, regular soldiers of the Roman army. They were responsible for the discipline of the regiment, and they were the cement which held the army together. In peace and in war alike, the morale of the Roman army depended on them. In his description of the Roman army, the Greek historian Polybius describes what a centurion should be: 'They must not be so much venturesome seekers after danger as men who can command, steady in action, and reliable; they ought not to be over-anxious to rush into the fight, but when hard pressed, they must be ready to hold their ground, and die at their posts.' The centurions were the finest men in the Roman army.

It is interesting to note that every centurion mentioned in the New Testament is mentioned with honour. There was the centurion who recognized Jesus on the cross as the Son of God; there was Cornelius, the first Gentile convert to the Christian Church; there was the centurion who suddenly discovered that Paul was a Roman citizen, and who rescued him from the fury of the rioting mob; there was the centurion who was informed that the Jews had planned to murder Paul between Jerusalem and Caesarea, and who took steps to foil their plans; there was the centurion whom Felix ordered to look after Paul; and there was the centurion accompanying Paul on his last journey to Rome, who treated him with every courtesy and accepted him as leader when the storm struck the ship (Matthew 27:54; Acts 10:22, 10:26, 22:26, 23:17, 23:23, 24:23, 27:3, 27:43). — William Barclay, *The Gospel of Matthew, Third Ed., The New Daily Study Bible* (Edinburgh: Saint Andrew Press, 2001), 347–348.

2. Now, let's read the story as a whole. What is surprising about this centurion?

But there was something very special about this centurion at Capernaum, and that was his attitude to his servant. This servant would be a slave, but the centurion was grieved that his servant was ill and was determined to do everything in his power to save him.

That was the reverse of the normal attitude of master to slave. In the Roman Empire, slaves did not matter. It was of no importance to anyone if they suffered and whether they lived or died. Aristotle, talking about the friendships which are possible in life, writes: 'There can be no friendship nor justice towards inanimate things; indeed, not even towards a horse or an ox, nor yet towards a slave as a slave. For master and slave have nothing in common: a slave is a living tool, just as a tool is an inanimate slave.'

A slave was no better than a thing. A slave had no legal rights whatsoever; his master was free to treat him, or maltreat him, as he liked. Gaius, the Roman legal expert, lays it down in his Institutes: 'We may note that it is universally accepted that the master possesses the power of life and death over the slave.' Varro, the Roman writer on agriculture, has a grim passage in which he divides the instruments of agriculture into three classes—the articulate, the inarticulate and the mute, 'the articulate comprising the slaves, the inarticulate comprising the cattle, and the mute comprising the vehicles'. The only difference between a slave and an animal or a cart was that the slave could speak. — William Barclay, *The Gospel of Matthew, Third Ed., The New Daily Study Bible* (Edinburgh: Saint Andrew Press, 2001), 348.

3. Is it surprising that this man would come to Jesus and this man would address Jesus as Lord? How so?

The second picture is in verses 5–13. Comprising this picture we find no less than seven surprises.

The first surprise is that "a centurion" approached Jesus (v. 5). Being a centurion meant two things, both very off-putting for Jews. First, he was a Gentile. He was not of the people of God. Second, he was part of the Roman military. He was oppressing the people of God. Thus, according to Jewish thinking, he was the wrong race and wore the wrong uniform.

The second surprise is that this centurion, who is under the lordship of Caesar, twice calls Jesus "Lord." "Lord" is the first word of his request (v. 6), and "Lord" is the first word of his reply (v. 8). Even if he is speaking better than he knows (which I don't think he is based on what he asks), again this word "Lord" in Matthew is significant symbolically. Believers call Jesus "Lord," while non-believers call him "teacher," "rabbi," etc. — Douglas Sean O'Donnell, *Matthew: All Authority in Heaven and on Earth, ed. R. Kent Hughes, Preaching the Word* (Wheaton, IL: Crossway, 2013), 206.

4. How did Jesus surprise this Centurion?

The fourth surprise is that Jesus responds to this request, saying, "I will come and heal him" (v. 7). It is surprising that Jesus doesn't say, "Well, let me first take a look at him and see if I can do anything for him." Rather he says, "I will come and heal him." It is also surprising (and this surprises the centurion) that Jesus is willing to enter a Gentile's house. Jews were prohibited from doing so. It was a cultural no-no. It would be similar to a white man sitting in the back of the bus or drinking from a "black only" drinking fountain in pre-civil rights America. Jesus was willing to cross over that line. — Douglas Sean O'Donnell, *Matthew: All Authority in Heaven and on Earth, ed. R. Kent Hughes, Preaching the Word* (Wheaton, IL: Crossway, 2013), 206–207.

5. Why does this man rebuff Jesus's request to come to his house?

The fifth surprise, however, is that this Gentile won't let him. "Lord," he says, "I am not worthy to have you come under my roof" (v. 8). In our next passage Jesus will say that he "has nowhere to lay his head" (8:20); he has no roof over his head, or at least none that he can call his own. What is so worthy about this homeless Jew?

Do you see the humility here? A Gentile, a military leader in the world's greatest army, a free Roman citizen, a man who has a household of slaves (which means he has some money) thinks Jesus is so worthy that it's unthinkable that our Lord should come over and just let himself in. It's like the Queen of England coming to town, meeting you on the street, and saying, "Oh, I'll just stay at your house tonight." What would you say to that? At first you would be honored. But then you'd come to your senses. And I don't care how upscale your house might be, you would suddenly recognize what a dump it is. "Oh, she can't stay here." That is this man's disposition. He is unworthy to have royalty—the Lord—into his house. — Douglas Sean O'Donnell, *Matthew: All Authority in Heaven and on Earth, ed. R. Kent Hughes, Preaching the Word* (Wheaton, IL: Crossway, 2013), 207.

6. How did the centurion surprise Jesus?

From there we come to the sixth surprise, found in verse 8–10: "Lord, I am not worthy to have you come under my roof, but only say the word, and my servant will be healed. For I too am a man under authority, with soldiers under me. And I say to one, 'Go,' and he goes, and to another, 'Come,' and he comes, and to my servant, 'Do this,' and he does it" (vv. 8, 9). "Just say a word, Jesus. I believe it will travel far enough, quickly enough, and powerfully enough to restore my servant."

"When Jesus heard this, he marveled and said to those who followed him, 'Truly, I tell you, with no one in Israel have I found such faith' " (v. 10). This sixth surprise—this man's faith—is what surprises Jesus. Jesus marveled that someone who didn't grow up like Paul, for example, learning the Torah, or even like Timothy with a Jewish mother and grandmother to teach him the Scriptures, knew enough to believe in Jesus and his word. This man expressed an "unlimited confidence in the authority of Jesus." You see, what Jesus is highlighting to his disciples, who were then all Jews, is that not even they "had shown the sincerity, sensitivity, humility, love, and depth of faith of this Gentile soldier." — Douglas Sean O'Donnell, *Matthew: All Authority in Heaven and on Earth, ed. R. Kent Hughes, Preaching the Word* (Wheaton, IL: Crossway, 2013), 207.

7. How would this story have surprised those who heard it in the first century?

The fact that contemporary Christian readers are accustomed to and comfortable with the notion of Gentile inclusion in God's people (without conversion to Judaism) should not dull our senses to the surprising nature of Jesus' words and Matthew's point. Although non-Jews would have been welcomed into Israel when they converted to Judaism (via circumcision and Torah obedience), an influx into the church of Gentiles who remain Gentiles was a surprising development within the early church (see Acts 10; 15). — Jeannine K. Brown, Matthew, ed. Mark L. Strauss and John H. Walton, *Teach the Text Commentary Series* (Grand Rapids, MI: Baker Books, 2015), 92–93.

8. What is the lesson in this story for us? What difference does it make?

The second miracle, the healing of the centurion's servant (8:5–13), is a reminder to us of Jesus' concern to extend the kingdom beyond the Jewish world. In his encounter with a Roman soldier, we again have the principle of Jesus reaching out that we saw when the wise men came to worship him as a child. All this anticipates the Great Commission to all the nations. What is interesting here is the centurion's great faith (v. 10), which contrasts with the disciples' 'little faith' (v. 26). Those whom we would expect to have great faith only have little faith, while those whom we might expect to have no faith at all show great trust in Jesus. For the centurion, Jesus heals the servant at a distance, rewarding the absolute confidence that the centurion puts in him. — Iain D. Campbell, *Opening up Matthew, Opening Up Commentary* (Leominster: Day One Publications, 2008), 56.

9. What do we learn about Christian living from this centurion's faith?

The text says that the centurion's faith took Jesus' breath away. In one translation, it says Jesus "marveled" at the centurion's assessment, a reaction I have found nowhere else in Scripture, regarding Jesus' impression of a human being's faith. This man had massive faith. Unwavering faith. The sort of just-say-the-word faith I covet for you and me.

Every time I read the account of the centurion's faith, I am nearly physically arrested by the desire to follow Christ like that. I want his influence to affect the entirety of my life—my values, my relationships, my vocabulary, my finances, my agenda, my physical health, my decision making, my political ideology. I want Jesus' ways to permeate who I am across the board. More than any other desire of my heart, I want to be a just-say-the-word type of disciple, from this moment until my dying day. — Bill Hybels, *The Power of a Whisper: Hearing God, Having the Guts to Respond* (Grand Rapids, MI: Zondervan, 2010).

10. What did this man know that every Christian needs to know?

According to this story, the faithful centurion understood his position, relative to Christ's. He also knew the profound power of a single whisper from God. "You just say the word," he essentially told Jesus Christ that day, "and what is wrong will be made right. You have authority over all people, over all rulers, over all events, over all kingdoms, over all of life. You say the word, and your will today will be done." — Bill Hybels, *The Power of a Whisper: Hearing God, Having the Guts to Respond* (Grand Rapids, MI: Zondervan, 2010).

11. Why do you suppose an outsider—a gentile— astonished Jesus with his faith, rather than, say, one of Jesus' own disciples?

Philip Yancey notes that there is something unpredictable about faith. Nine times in the Gospels Jesus says to people, "Your faith has healed you." But he often praises faith in unlikely people. In fact, often it is foreigners who show the greatest faith. A Roman centurion tells Jesus that Jesus does not even need to come to his home to perform a healing; he believes that all Jesus has to do is speak a word and it will be so. Jesus is amazed: "I have not found anyone in Israel with such great faith," he says (Matthew 8:10). A Canaanite woman pesters Jesus to help her daughter when Jesus is on retreat. He seems to put her off, reminding her that he was sent to the lost sheep of Israel and not the Gentile "dogs." But she persists in this strange tug-of-war until Jesus gives in or perhaps allows to be revealed in her what he knew was there all along, exclaiming, "Woman, you have great faith!" (Matthew 15:28). Why does faith so often thrive where it is least expected? Why do suffering and persecution — intended to destroy faith — so often strengthen it instead? — John Ortberg, *Know Doubt: Embracing Uncertainty in Your Faith* (Grand Rapids, MI: Zondervan, 2014).

12. What did this man have going for him? What was going well in his life?

Keep in mind that the Romans had conquered Israel and were therefore the despised occupiers of the land. Furthermore, to attain the position of centurion, one had to prove himself a valiant warrior in battle. Therefore, the centurion in this story was not merely a soldier in the occupying forces—he was a commanding officer. We also know, from Luke's account of the same incident, that he was wealthy.

So, in the passage before us, Matthew paints a picture of a wealthy Roman approaching a poor Galilean, a powerful centurion seeking out a meek Carpenter, a mighty man of war addressing the Prince of Peace. — Jon Courson, *Jon Courson's Application Commentary* (Nashville, TN: Thomas Nelson, 2003), 58.

13. What was not well in his life?

IT troubles you, fatigues you, shames you. IT is the disease you can't heal, the job you can't stomach, the marriage you can't fix, the rage you can't tame.

IT hurts.

IT looms over life. Two towering letters, tall and defiant. IT! They march like Frankenstein's monster. Each step a thud. Each thud an earthquake. Clomp. Clomp. Clomp. IT! IT! IT!

"Look out! Here IT comes!"

"I can't take IT anymore!"

IT overshadows and intimidates everyone—everyone, that is, except people who take IT to Jesus. People like the Roman soldier.

He was a centurion. He held unquestioned authority over his men. Yet there was something special about this particular officer. He loved his servant. " 'Lord, my servant is lying at home paralyzed, dreadfully tormented.' And Jesus said to him, 'I will come and heal him' " (Matt. 8:6–7).

The soldier's prayer was unembroidered. He simply stated a fact: "My servant is lying at home paralyzed, dreadfully tormented."

That was enough to set Jesus in motion. He turned and immediately began to walk in the direction of the centurion's house. — Max Lucado, *Before Amen: The Power of a Simple Prayer* (Nashville: Thomas Nelson, 2014).

14. How would readers in the first century have felt about this man as he is introduced in the story?

A second petitioner approaches Jesus as he is returning home to Capernaum. Again the identity of the supplicant is crucial. The centurion would have been a Gentile, the commander of a division of the occupying imperial troops, theoretically one hundred in number. Orthodox Jews would have considered the centurion unclean because of his race and despised him all the more as a symbol of Roman subjugation. — Craig Blomberg, *Matthew, vol. 22, The New American Commentary* (Nashville: Broadman & Holman Publishers, 1992), 140.

15. What do we learn about faith from this story?

Even those who were his disciples needed to learn the importance of absolute confidence in Jesus. While the centurion trusted the ability of an absent Christ, the disciples could not trust the power of a present Christ. The miracle of the calming of the storm was a means of showing to them the absolute power of Christ over all of nature; but more than this, it was a confirmation to their weak faith of his glory and of the majesty of his kingly person (see John's statement in John 2:11 that when Jesus turned the water into wine, he 'manifested his glory [and] his disciples believed in him'). — Iain D. Campbell, *Opening up Matthew, Opening Up Commentary* (Leominster: Day One Publications, 2008), 56–57.

16. What is the application of this story to our lives?

The challenge for today's Christian is to ask: what does it mean to recognize, and submit to, the authority of Jesus himself? What does it mean to call him 'Lord' and live by that? There is nothing in the New Testament to suggest that 'faith' is a general awareness of a supernatural dimension, or a general trust in the goodness of some distant divinity, so that some might arrive at this through Jesus and others by some quite different route. 'Faith', in Christian terms, means believing precisely that the living God has entrusted his authority to Jesus himself, who is now exercising it for the salvation of the world (see 28:18). If the policeman used his authority to break up a student party, Jesus is using his to set in motion a much greater celebration. And he invites us all to share in it. — Tom Wright, *Matthew for Everyone, Part 1: Chapters 1-15* (London: Society for Promoting Christian Knowledge, 2004), 85.

17. This man's faith was the conduit through which the miracle flowed. Jesus said in another place, "It will be done for you according to your faith." Why do you think God choose faith as the conduit for miracles? Why not righteousness or love or acts of compassion?

On one occasion, Jesus found himself being chased by two blind men. They followed him indoors. The first thing Jesus said to them was, "Do you believe I am able to do this?" (Matthew 9:28) Strange way to start a conversation. There seemed to be an understanding that everyone knew what he was talking about when he said, "Do you believe I am able to do this?" Jesus went on to explain that this was not a rhetorical question. He really wanted to know. Everything depended on whether they believed—really believed—that Jesus could touch their eyes and they would look out the window and see their first-ever sunset. "According to your faith it will be done for you," Jesus said flatly. "You make the call," Jesus was saying. If you want to be healed, you can be. But you must believe it to see it. It will be done for you according to your faith.

I believe the eyes of the Lord are moving back and forth across the whole earth (2 Chronicles 16:9) to find a people of faith, because nothing happens until someone believes. I believe God would still say to his people, as he said to those two blind men, "It will be done for you according to your faith." You will see it when you believe it.

Dreams are about faith. They are about seeing what is invisible until it becomes visible. Dreams and faith are the conduit of all God's activity on earth. God is not limited to our faith, but he often chooses to limit his power to match the faith of people. Jesus did not do many miracles in his hometown, "Because of their lack of faith." (Matthew 13:58) Notice it does not say he could not do many miracles, just that he did not. He can do anything. God often chooses to trace along the lines of our faith. — Josh Hunt, *You Can Double Your Church In Five Years or Less*, 2000.

18. Why is faith such a big deal to God? Why did this man's faith impress Jesus so?

Faith, or trust, is at the center of every healthy relationship. As trust goes, so goes the relationship. A break in trust signals a break in the relationship. Sin was introduced to the world through a choice not to trust. In the Garden of Eden, humanity's relationship with God was broken when Eve and Adam quit trusting. God has been on a quest ever since to reengage with mankind in a relationship characterized by trust. The entire Old Testament is the story of God saying, "Trust me." It's no coincidence that God didn't give Israel the law until they first learned to trust him and follow him. With that as a backdrop, we shouldn't be surprised to discover that at the epicenter of Jesus' message was the word believe. Just as humankind's relationship with God was destroyed through a lack of faith, so it would be restored through an expression of the same. At its core, Christianity is an invitation to reenter a relationship of trust with the Father. At the cross, sin was forgiven and we were invited to trust. It makes perfect sense that salvation comes by faith, not obedience. Intimate relationships are not built on obedience. They are built on trust. Walking by faith, again, is simply living as if God is who he says he is and that he will do everything he has promised to do. As a person's confidence in God grows, he or she matures.

As we continued our discussion, we talked about the Christians we knew who appeared to have the strongest relationships with Christ. In every case, these were men and women with big faith — extraordinary confidence in God in spite of what life threw at them. These were the people whose faith amazed us. I was convinced then, as I am now, that God is most honored through living, active, death-defying, out-of-the-box faith. During one of these discussions, someone on our team pointed out that the only time Jesus was ever "amazed" was when he saw expressions of great faith and little faith. Big faith was a big deal to Jesus. When people acted on what they believed about him, he was impressed. We are as well. Isn't it true that we love the stories about people in our church who trust God against all odds? We revel in the accounts of teenagers who decide to live out their values at school because they believe God's promises. What about those hospital visits when you walk in praying for the right thing to say, and you are greeted by a family whose faith in God is staggering? They are confident. No fear. I don't know about you, but there have been plenty of times when I have driven home from a hospital visit wondering why they let me be the pastor. As I write, I'm reminded of a couple in our small group that has two children with severe vision impairment. I've heard Chris and Dave share their story on three occasions. Each time I am moved to tears when I hear Chris talk about their confidence in God through a series of difficult conversations with doctors and two very difficult pregnancies. Maggie and Luke suffer from different conditions, both of which have left them legally blind. — Andy Stanley, *Deep and Wide: Creating Churches Unchurched People Love to Attend* (Grand Rapids, MI: Zondervan, 2012).

19. How do we enlarge the conduit of faith so God can do greater works in our lives? How do we become people of great faith and confidence?

Another crucial clue for understanding our lives with God is to realize that faith is his gift to us. We can't scrunch it into existence. We received that gift when we received him into our hearts and lives for salvation. With salvation came faith to believe. Without faith, we would not have it in our hearts to receive Jesus in the first place. In our natural selves, we would be indifferent to the spiritual light, which is Jesus. Why? The sinner prefers darkness. So no one who knows

Christ can say, "I have no faith." Faith is part of the salvation package.

Do you fear that your faith is too poor or weak? Remember this, all faith, no matter how poor or weak, serves as our conduit . . . our contact to the source of our faith, who is Christ Jesus, who is not small or feeble.

Our faith depends on our choices. We can will in our spirits to grow, develop, and mature in that God-given faith by eating the "food" found in Scripture. Everything we need for healthy faith-growth is in the Bible. We may eat all we can hold and not gain weight. If you supplement with chocolate . . . that's your choice. —MARILYN MEBERG (*God at Your Wits' End*) / Various Authors, *Patchwork Devotional: 365 Snippets of Inspiration, Joy, and Hope* (Nashville: Thomas Nelson, 2010).

20. What blessings come to those of big faith?

Big faith is a necessity in every chapter. But the expressions of that faith will change with time.

The teenagers in your church need a faith that is strong enough to endure the challenges of adolescence. Your college students need faith that's big enough to enable them to trust God with their futures. The singles in your church face a different set of challenges than either of those groups. The married couples in your church need to know they can trust God with their spouses and children. The seniors in your church need to know they can trust God during a stage of life when losing loved ones is commonplace and every day brings new reminders of their mortality. — Andy Stanley, *Deep and Wide: Creating Churches Unchurched People Love to Attend* (Grand Rapids, MI: Zondervan, 2012).

21. Here is one you will have to think about. What is even more important than having big faith?

It's better to have little faith in a big God than to have big faith in a little god. That's why Jesus said we just need faith like a mustard seed.

I once heard pastor and author Tim Keller speaking about the Israelites' escape from Egypt. As Pharaoh came after them, God parted the Red Sea, and the Israelites crossed over on dry ground. Most likely some of them were reveling in it: "In your face, Pharaoh! We're cruising now!"

But at the same time, others were probably saying, "We're all gonna die! We're all gonna die!"

It's not the quality of our faith that saves us, Tim said. It's the object of our faith.

This is why Paul wedges in this description of the God Abraham believed in: "[Abraham] is our father in the sight of God, in whom he believed —the God who gives life to the dead and calls into being things that were not" (Romans 4:17). The character of Abraham's faith is determined by the character of the God in whom he believed.[15]

It turns out you don't YOLO after all. The only thing God needed to get this redemption project going was Abraham's trust. Not perfection. Not superhuman efforts. Simple trust. God can work with that.

The worst year in my life was maybe the best in my wife's. I had lived for many months with a deep depression and a feeling of pain that would not go away. It seemed clear to me that my life's work would continually be less effective. At the same time, Nancy had taken a new full-time job and was soaring with a level of energy and joy I had never seen in her before.

I can remember lying in bed at night, listening to her having meetings downstairs in our home with the staff she led, hearing laughter and enthusiasm and planning happening recreationally —and being thoroughly miserable. Her energized success made my own painful inadequacy look that much darker. I found myself quite envious.

One night while I was wrestling with this, a question entered my mind: Do I want to be the kind of man who needs his wife to be less successful so he can feel better about himself?

I lay still for several minutes, hoping for an easier question.

But I knew the answer. Many things were unclear to me, but I knew I did not want to be the kind of person who needs his spouse to look smaller so he can feel bigger.

And in a strange way, seeing that weakness and neediness in myself was the beginning of healing. Ernest Kurtz writes in The Spirituality of Imperfection that, ironically, perfectionism is the great enemy of spiritual growth. An ancient sage named Macarius used to point out that if all we did was make progress, we would become conceited, and conceit is the ultimate downfall of Christians. — John Ortberg, *All the Places You'll Go . . . except When You Don't: God Has Placed before You an Open Door. What Will You Do?* (Carol Stream, IL: Tyndale, 2015).

22. How can we support one another in prayer this week?

What Happens When Group Members Commit to Pray for One Another?

- Your relationship with Christ and with each other will deepen. You will experience spiritual growth.

- There is less chance of burnout as you put problems in God's hands and trust members to his care.

- You allow the Holy Spirit to work in your group so your time together is filling and refreshing.

- God will answer your prayers in amazing ways, and your faith will increase. http://www.smallgroups.com/articles/2012/facilitate-meaningful-group-prayer.html

Lesson #10, Matthew 9.35 – 10.8

Good Questions Have Groups Talking
www.joshhunt.com

Matthew 9.35 – 10.8

OPEN

Let's each share your name and, have you ever been on a mission trip? In a sentence or two, tell us about it.

DIG

1. What do we learn about ourselves from this passage?

As a good shepherd, Jesus looked at humanity's lost sheep who were scattered, frightened, and hungry. What He saw pulled at His heartstrings. He was full of tenderness for them. He had compassion for them. Just as these hurting people touched the heart of the Savior, so should hurting people today touch our hearts. — Charles R. Swindoll, *Bedside Blessings* (Nashville: Thomas Nelson, 2002).

2. What does it mean that we are like sheep? What is a sheep like?

In today's busy, increasingly urban world, many people do not know basic facts about farm animals. If you know something about them, test your knowledge about sheep with these statements, answering true or false.

___ Sheep are able to seek out their own sources of food and water.

___ Sheep help one another when a sheep is wounded or stuck.

___ Sheep are strong and able to carry packs on their back.

___ Sheep are not afraid to graze away from the herd.

___ Sheep will follow anyone who gives them a command.

If you answered true to any of these, you're wrong! The actual characteristics of sheep are the exact opposite of the ones described here. When Jesus said that we are like sheep, He was not paying us a high compliment.

Sheep are simpleminded, but they respond immediately to the love and tender care of their shepherd—and only their shepherd. Jesus said, "The sheep hear his [the shepherd's] voice, and he calls his own sheep by name, and leads them out. When he puts forth all his own, he goes before them, and the sheep follow him because they know his voice" (John 10:3–4 NASB).

The sheep have security and direction because they know their shepherd and respond to his commands. Do you know your Shepherd's voice? — Charles F. Stanley, *On Holy Ground* (Nashville, TN: Thomas Nelson Publishers, 1999), 326.

3. **A good cross-reference is Psalm 23. What do we learn about sheep from this classic Psalm? What do we learn about ourselves?**

The Lord does have a special relationship with those who love him and seek him, who walk in his ways and desire what he desires. God never promises that we'll have trouble-free lives, but he does promise that we'll never face anything that comes our way alone. Sometimes we forget that all we have to do is ask God for wisdom when life gets complicated, when we're confused, or when we're making a hard decision. Jesus said, "Ask and you will receive" (John 16:24, NIV).

The Twenty-third Psalm is a great psalm of comfort and hope. "The LORD is my shepherd; I shall not want" (Psalm

23:1, NKJV). As you read the entire psalm, it's more than just sweet sentiments. It's a list, a strong list of promises that cover every need and every phase of life from being hungry to dying.

Think of the phrase "thy rod and thy staff they comfort me" (Psalm 23:4, KJV). Both the rod and staff are tools to protect us, not just from predators but also from ourselves. We, like sheep, are prone to wander. A good shepherd needs to firmly strike a stubborn sheep, but for those sheep who love to stay near him, a little tap is all that's needed. — Debbi Bryson, *The One Year Wisdom for Women Devotional: 365 Devotions through the Proverbs* (Carol Stream, IL: Tyndale, 2013).

4. What do we learn about prayer from this passage?

Journal Entry, December 7, 1944

"Wonderful time on the hill last night. Asked the Lord that he might work in the hearts of high school, college kids, or business people to the end that in years to come HE would give us out of the whole US top-notchers for the work He is going to do through The Navigators. Might just as well put it down in my book now that it is a settled matter, the Lord accepted my request. It is on His books and on the way."

On December 6, 1944, Dawson Trotman left his home after dinner to climb the bluffs behind his home at 509 Monterey Road. He took his jacket, Bible, and a Navy blanket and climbed the hill to a favorite spot where he could see the city lights.

After reflecting on the new staff members that the Lord had brought The Navigators, he began to pray for future generations of laborers. Dawson's work in boys and girls Bible clubs and at BIOLA had taught him the importance of training youth, and he was beginning to see the fruits of his ministry. That December night he prayed that the Lord would raise up young laborers for the field, and he was confident that the Lord would do it.

More than sixty-five years later, it is easy to see how faithfully and abundantly God answered Trotman's prayer on the hill behind his house. The staff of The Navigators has grown from 4 in 1944 to over 4,800 in 2011. The Navigators has laborers all over the globe, in 108 countries. — Ken Albert et al., *Dawson Trotman: In His Own Words* (Colorado Springs, CO: NavPress, 2011).

5. What do we learn about the bottleneck to the evangelistic / disciplemaking process? Why aren't there more disciples than there are?

Faith without works is dead.

Dreaming, believing, setting goals. . . these are all well and good. Ultimately, what gets things done is work. Every good idea degenerates into work.

The bottleneck of the evangelistic process has always been laborers (Matthew 9:37). A laborer is someone who works. Faith is important. Dreaming is important. Believing is important. So is doing. What we do when we get off our knees is every bit as important as the prayer of faith.

Jesus told his disciples to watch and pray (Matthew 26:41). He also told them to "Rise, let us go!" (Matthew 26:46) There is a time for everything. A time to pray and a time to act. A time to dream and a time to sweat. (See Ecclesiastes 3) When Peter saw Jesus transfigured he wanted to set up camp. Jesus reminded him there was work to do in the valley.

Paul admonished us to, "Not become weary in doing good." (Galatians 6:9) There is a not-so-subtle implication that their ought to be a temptation to grow weary. Someone who is never tempted to grow weary in doing good is probably being disobedient to something. Paul said a similar thing to the Thessalonians: "And as for you, brothers, never tire of doing what is right." (II Thessalonians 3:13) I think we ought to occasionally wander close to tiring of doing what is right. Never actually tiring of the work, but feeling the temptation of fatigue from time to time. I have observed many pastors who seemed to know too much about gardening and golf and not enough about leadership and preparing outstanding sermons. — Josh Hunt, *You Can Double Your Church In Five Years or Less*, 2000.

6. One of the things to look for as you study Scripture is to ask, "What would I have expected this verse to say." In this case, I would have expected this verse to tell us to pray for the lost. (By the way, I think praying for the lost is a good thing.) Why do you think Jesus asked us to pray for workers, rather than praying for the lost? What is the lesson for us?

Leadership was the emphasis. Jesus had already demonstrated by his own ministry that the deluded masses were ripe for the harvest, but without spiritual shepherds to lead them, how could they ever be won? "Pray ye therefore the Lord of the harvest," Jesus reminded his disciples, "that he will send forth laborers into his harvest" (Matt. 9:37–38; see Luke 10:2). There is almost a note of desperation in these words—a desperation wrung from the sense of the world's desperate need of workers with them who cared for their souls. There is no use to pray for the world. What good would it do? God already loves them and has given his Son to save them. No, there is no use to pray vaguely for the world. The world is lost and blind in sin. The only hope for the world is for laborers to go to them with the gospel of salvation, and having won them to the Savior, not to leave them, but to work with them faithfully, patiently, painstakingly, until they become fruitful Christians savoring the world about them with the Redeemer's love. — Robert E. Coleman, *The Master Plan of Evangelism* (Grand Rapids, MI: Revell, 2006), 93–94.

7. How did Jesus see crowds of people differently than we do? What do we learn about being Christlike from this passage?

What do we see? "When [Jesus] saw the multitudes, He was moved with compassion for them, because they were weary and scattered, like sheep having no shepherd" (Matthew 9:36). . . .

Let's be the people who look at the hurting until we hurt with them. No hurrying past, turning away, or shifting of eyes. No pretending or glossing over. Let's look at the face until we see the person.

A family in our congregation lives with the heartbreaking reality that their son is homeless. He ran away when he was seventeen, and with the exception of a few calls from prison and one visit, they have had no contact with him for twenty years. The mom allowed me to interview her at a leadership gathering. As we prepared for the discussion, I asked her why she was willing to disclose her story.

"I want to change the way people see the homeless. I want them to stop seeing problems and begin seeing mothers' sons."

Change begins with a genuine look. And continues with a helping hand.

Works done in God's name long outlive our earthly lives. — OUTLIVE YOUR LIFE / Max Lucado, *Live Loved: Experiencing God's Presence in Everyday Life* (Nashville: Thomas Nelson, 2011).

8. Jesus told us quite specifically to pray for workers in the harvest. Yet, at most prayer meetings I have attended, it is rare to hear this prayer voiced. Why do you suppose this is? Why do you think we don't pray more regularly for workers?

Today Jesus continues to say, "The harvest is plentiful but the workers are few. Ask the Lord of the harvest, therefore, to send out workers into his harvest field" (Matthew 9:37–38, NIV). Notice that Jesus does not say to pray for more observers or more spectators or more complainers. He is asking that you pray for more laborers.

But no one can honestly pray that prayer if he or she is not willing to do it him- or herself. Unfortunately, it seems like the church today could be compared to a giant football game, with sixty thousand people in the stands watching while twenty-two people do all the work. We all stand on the sidelines and say, "Go, team! Go!" But God is saying, "I want you down on the field. I want you to carry the ball. I want you to be a part of what I am doing."

You may feel unqualified for the calling, but think of what Jesus did with the twelve disciples. When we think of these men, we often think of them as holy or special. Yet though they were gifted and dedicated, they were ordinary. Jesus did not call them because they were great. Their greatness was the result of the call of Jesus.

God wants to use you. He has a place for you, a part for you to play, a seed for you to sow, a call for you to answer. Begin by asking God's Holy Spirit to stir your heart so that you can answer this desire and wish of Jesus. You may pray something like this: "Lord, let it start with me. Make me a laborer—a fisher of men and women in this sea of life. I don't know what I can do. I feel a bit like that kid in the Bible who just had the loaves and fish. Here is my lunch, Lord—it's not much, but I give it to you." If you pray that type of heartfelt prayer, just watch what God will do! — Greg Laurie, *New Believer's Guide to How to Share Your Faith* (Carol Stream, IL: Tyndale House Publishers, Inc., 1999), 73–74.

9. What percentage of Christians would you say are workers?

A survey among evangelical Christians revealed that 95 percent of those polled had never led another person to Christ. Yet Jesus gave us His marching orders. He said, "Go therefore and make disciples of all the nations, baptizing them in the name of the Father and of the Son and of the Holy Spirit, teaching them to observe all things that I have commanded you ..." (Matt. 28:19–20). This is an order from our Commander in Chief, and it isn't merely addressed to pastors or missionaries. It's addressed to every man or woman who names the name of Christ. — Greg Laurie, *For Every Season, Volume Two* (Dana Point, CA: Kerygma Publishing—Allen David Books, 2011).

10. Does God ever raise up workers if we don't pray? Does God ever do anything except in response to prayer?

I scoured the New Testament some time ago, looking for things God does in ministry that are not prompted by prayer. Do you know what I found?

Nothing.

I don't mean I had trouble finding an item or two; I mean I found nothing. Everything God does in the work of ministry, He does through prayer. Consider:

• Prayer is the way you defeat the devil (Luke 22:32; James 4:7).

• Prayer is the way you get the lost saved (Luke 18:13).

• Prayer is the way you acquire wisdom (James 1:5).

• Prayer is the way a backslider gets restored (James 5:16–20).

• Prayer is how the saints get strengthened (Jude 20, Matthew 26:41).

• Prayer is the way we get laborers out to the mission field (Matthew 9:38).

• Prayer is how we cure the sick (James 5:13–15).

• Prayer is how we accomplish the impossible (Mark 11:23–24).

I could go on listing the myriad divine activities initiated by prayer, but I suspect you get the point. Everything we do that's worth doing; everything God wants to do in the church; everything God wants to do in your life; He has subjugated it all to one thing: Prayer. I am reminded of a little paradigm I heard years ago that embodies a crucial truth concerning our prayer lives:

What we do for the Lord is entirely dependent upon what we receive from the Lord, and what we receive from the Lord is entirely dependent upon what we are in the Lord, and what we are in the Lord is entirely dependent upon the time we spend alone with the Lord in prayer.

It is impossible for us to do or to be anything that God wants us to do or be, apart from spending time in the prayer closet. — David Jeremiah, *Prayer: The Great Adventure* (Sisters, OR: Multnomah Publishers, 1997), 40–41.

11. Why do you think many are reluctant be serve? Why the worker shortage?

Brian encouraged me to apply what I was learning. At the time I met Brian, I was also attending a college-age group at church. They needed a song leader. I was reluctant to volunteer since I had only been playing the guitar for six months, but Brian encouraged me to try. With my knees knocking, I got up in front of the eighty-plus students and learned to lead songs. He started coming to the meetings to encourage me afterward. He enabled me to take a risk, and through it I was learning to serve Jesus. — *Discipleship Journal, Issue 67* (January/February 1992) (NavPress, 1992).

12. What benefits come to workers that don't come to those who are not engaged in the work?

One man wrote: My life used to be about one thing: me. I was a self-serving guy who had neither purpose nor passion. I was leading a miserable life, throwing away time and money on beer and cheap thrills. Then one day I walked into a church and heard the message of Christ: Give your life away to others and you will find your life. I didn't have much to give up so I decided to give it a shot.

That's when my life started to change and Christ became more real to me. I started serving teenagers and found a purpose . . . a reason for my existence.

It was twenty-one years ago that I wandered into that church. Today my life is richer than I ever believed it could be. Serving others made the difference. It was one of the best decisions I ever made. — Bill Hybels, *The Volunteer Revolution: Unleashing the Power of Everybody* (Grand Rapids, MI: Zondervan, 2009).

13. Here is one just to think about: how often do you pray for workers in the harvest of our town?

That means we have to ask ourselves practical questions about where our prayer focus is. Whose thoughts are we thinking when we pray? In our church prayer meeting, is it all about small things—personal things, things to do with us and our present health or circumstances, or whatever else? Is that true in our personal prayers, in our family prayers? Or is it always, whatever we're praying for, undergirded by a focus on the great issues of Christ and his coming kingdom, on thinking God's thoughts after him? — William Philip and Alistair Begg, *Why We Pray* (Wheaton, IL: Crossway, 2015).

14. Let's pause and pray that God would raise up workers for the harvest in our town.

So prayer is indispensable to the work of ministry, both in our personal lives and in the life of the church. The natural question then arises: Was prayer as central to the early church? Was it as important in the beginning as we understand it to be today? The best place to answer that question is to scan the book of Acts, which tells the story of the early church.

And what we find is that Acts is a veritable handbook on prayer. Everywhere you turn, the disciples are praying— and remarkable things are happening in response. This is true from the very first chapter. Immediately following the Lord's ascension, the disciples returned to Jerusalem and congregated in an "upper room." Luke lists all the people who were present, all those who would make up the leadership and foundation of the church. Then he says, "these all with one mind were continually devoting themselves to prayer...." That was the foundation of the church; it all got started through prayer. And that was even before Pentecost! —

David Jeremiah, *Prayer: The Great Adventure* (Sisters, OR: Multnomah Publishers, 1997), 41–42.

15. Matthew 10.1 – 8. Summarize Jesus' instructions to the apostles?

Four things stand out in this commissioning passage:

The work Jesus gives his people to do (vv. 5–15)

The place of their work is to be among 'the lost sheep of the house of Israel' (v. 6). We have already seen that Matthew is preparing the way for the universal proclamation of the gospel—wise men from the east have already worshipped Jesus and a Roman soldier has been commended for his faith. One day, disciples will be made in all the nations (28:19). But Jesus is reflecting the unique purpose of God in the mission to the world—Israel is the light of all the nations (see Isa. 42:6; 49:6; 60:3). God 'had chosen Israel in relation to his purpose for the world, not just for Israel'. Yet there was still much that had to be accomplished in Israel up until the death, resurrection and ascension of Jesus. Only after Pentecost would the Christian mission extend among the Gentiles and the Samaritans.

The content of their work is to continue proclaiming the message that Jesus himself has preached: 'The kingdom of heaven is at hand' (v. 7). Like his teaching, theirs is to be accompanied and authenticated by miracles of healing, resurrection and exorcism.

The provision for their work is to be met entirely by God himself. They are to take no gold or silver, no excess baggage, no staff. God will make provision for them through the hospitality of those who will receive their message. The apostles are to approach all communities in peaceable ways and for peaceful purposes. If they are not received, they are to withdraw. God will deal with the hard-hearted cities who refuse to come to him, just as he will make provision for those who serve him. — Iain D. Campbell, *Opening up Matthew, Opening Up Commentary* (Leominster: Day One Publications, 2008), 63–64.

16. Verse 2. For the first time, the disciples are called apostles. What exactly is an apostle?

Matthew takes this opportunity to give us a list of the Twelve themselves, calling them for the first time 'apostles', that is, people who are 'sent out', as Jesus was now sending them, and would later send all those who witnessed his resurrection. The number 12 is itself of course full of meaning, as anyone in Jesus' world would recognize; at the heart of what Jesus was up to was his belief that through his work God was at last renewing and restoring Israel, which traditionally had been based upon the twelve tribes. But now the Twelve were not just to be a sign that God was restoring Israel; they were to be part of the means by which he was doing so. — Tom Wright, *Matthew for Everyone, Part 1: Chapters 1-15* (London: Society for Promoting Christian Knowledge, 2004), 111–112.

17. Matthew 10.5. Why not go to the Gentiles? What is the lesson for us?

The kind of fish you want to catch will determine every part of your strategy. Fishing for bass, catfish, or salmon requires different equipment, bait, and timing. You don't catch marlin the same way you catch trout. There is no "one-size-fits-all" approach to fishing. Each demands a unique strategy. The same is true in fishing for men—it helps to know what you're fishing for!

When Jesus sent his disciples out on their first evangelistic campaign, he defined the target very specifically: They were to focus on their own countrymen. "These twelve Jesus sent out with the following instructions: 'Do not go among the Gentiles or enter any town of the Samaritans. Go rather to the lost sheep of Israel' " (Matt. 10:5–6).

There may have been several reasons Jesus narrowed the target, but one thing is certain: He targeted the kind of people the disciples were most likely to reach—people like themselves. Jesus was not being prejudiced, he was being strategic. As I mentioned in chapter 9, Jesus defined the disciples' target so they'd be effective, not in order to be exclusive. — Rick Warren, *The Purpose Driven Church: Growth without Compromising Your Message and Mission* (Grand Rapids, MI: Zondervan, 2007).

18. Verse 7. What was the gospel as Jesus proclaimed it?

So, what did the early church understand the gospel to be, and how does it differ from the way we see it? More importantly, what was the gospel as Jesus actually communicated it?

John Ortberg posed this question as the opening statement in a message he did at the Arts Conference at Willowcreek several years ago. I have listened to it so many times that I don't really know any more where John Ortberg's thoughts on the subject stop and mine start. I just know that I owe a huge dept of gratitude to John Ortberg for helping me understand this topic. This article is more or less a paraphrase of that message. I can't blame everything I am going to say on John Ortberg, but I do want to give credit where credit is due.

(You can listen to a similar lesson called "The offer that changes everything." at http://www.mppc.org/esermons. html?next_page=3&curr_page=2 or, purchase the Willowcreek message by doing a search for "Arts Conference 2003: Imagine Life in the Kingdom" at www.willowcreek.com)

Back to the question: what is the gospel? Ask the average church goer today and they would describe the plan to get to heaven. To use a metaphor, it might go something like this. It is like a house. When you first come into the house, there is a grand staircase in the front entry way. It is lit by a huge, ornate chandelier. It has bright red carpet. All the architectural clues invite you to come upstairs. There must be something wonderful upstairs. And you begin to talk to the residents, and you find it is true. Upstairs is a place where there is love and joy and peace and all the good things in life. But, the residents tell you, that staircase does not lead you there. It may appear to lead you there, but it is a dead end. It does not. It leads only to disappointment and frustration.

The downstairs represents earth. The upstairs represents heaven. The staircase represents works, which feel like they ought to get us to heaven. The message of the gospel is that they don't. There is an old simple-looking stair case out back. It doesn't look like much, but it will take you upstairs. It will lead you to heaven. It is called grace. You must have faith in the staircase called grace to get to heaven. That is the gospel.

The gospel of the modern church, but is it the gospel of Jesus? Is it the gospel of the early church? Is this really a summary of the message that Jesus proclaimed when he taught? Look at these verses.

- After John was put in prison, Jesus went into Galilee, proclaiming the good news of God. "The time has come," he said. "The kingdom of God is near. Repent and believe the good news!" Mark 1:14-15 [NIV]

- After this, Jesus traveled about from one town and village to another, proclaiming the good news of the kingdom of God. Luke 8:1 [NIV]

- When Jesus had called the Twelve together, he gave them power and authority to drive out all demons and to cure diseases, and he sent them out to preach the kingdom of God and to heal the sick. Luke 9:1-2 [NIV]

- After his suffering, he showed himself to these men and gave many convincing proofs that he was alive. He appeared to them over a period of forty days and spoke about the kingdom of God. Acts 1:3 [NIV]

- Boldly and without hindrance he preached the kingdom of God and taught about the Lord Jesus Christ. Acts 28:31 [NIV]

What was the gospel that Jesus himself spoke? What was the gospel that electrified the early church and caused it to explode in growth? It was not primarily about how to get to heaven when you die. It was all about the kingdom. http://www.joshhunt.com/mail145.htm

19. What exactly is the Kingdom of God?

The word kingdom is a little obscure to us, but it was common in that day, and it is a common, very human, concept. Everyone has a kingdom. A kingdom is that sphere where what you say goes. John Ortberg quotes Dallas Willard with the definition, "It is the range of your effective will." It is that little circle that you control--what you say goes.

Kingdoms are very important to us, even as children. Two of the early words that kids learn are, "Mine," meaning, "This is part of my kingdom, and, "No," an indication that you have violated the child's kingdom.

In God's kingdom, we find things like love, joy, peace, patience, kindness, goodness, gentleness, faithfulness and self-control. When God is in charge, that is what we find. In man's kingdom, we find quite the opposite--things like hatred and discord and sadness and bitterness and envy and discontentment and unfaithfulness and so forth. Watch an episode of Law and Order and you find a good example of the kingdom of this world.

Jesus taught us to pray, "Thy kingdom come. Thy will be done, on earth, as it is in heaven." His message was not primarily that we could go to heaven when we die, and that was by grace through faith. That is a message we often hear in church, but Jesus didn't talk about that much. Jesus' message was about the idea that the kingdom of God is available, right here right now in your work, in your home, on your cul-de-sac, on your Monday morning.

The message of Jesus was not primarily about the secret staircase out back that leads upstairs to the treasures that are there. It is about the fact that those treasures upstairs are available downstairs. The message of the gospel is that we can live a life that is largely characterized by love, joy, peace, patience, kindness, goodness, gentleness, faithfulness and self control. Right here. Right now. Today. That life is available to you.

http://www.joshhunt.com/mail145.htm

20. Why do you think Jesus sent the twelve out? What was He planning for this experience to do for the disciples?

'But how will I know the way?' I asked, setting off on my first solo car journey.

'Don't be silly,' said my mother. 'We've been going there for years! You'll know it all right.'

But I didn't. I recognized many parts of the road. But there is all the difference in the world between sitting in a car, while someone else makes the decisions about which road to take, and doing it yourself. I got lost—just five miles from my own home!—and had to backtrack and ask someone for directions, as though I were a stranger in the area.

Up until this moment, Jesus' disciples have been passengers in the car, and he's been doing the driving. They have been astonished at what they've seen, but he's made all the decisions, handled all the tricky moments, steered them through the towns and villages, taken the criticisms, and come out in front. Now he's telling them to go off and do it themselves. It doesn't take much imagination to see how they would feel. You want us to do it? By ourselves? — Tom Wright, *Matthew for Everyone, Part 1: Chapters 1-15 (London: Society for Promoting Christian Knowledge*, 2004), 111.

21. What do you want to recall from today's conversation?

22. How can we support one another in prayer this week?

Lesson #11, Matthew 11.20 - 30
Good Questions Have Groups Talking
www.joshhunt.com

Matthew 11.20 - 30

OPEN

Let's each share your name and, how often do you take a nap?

DIG

1. **Matthew 11.20 – 24. What do we learn about being Christlike from this passage?**

   But long before the first western was ever made, Jesus overturned the tables in the temple. Money flew, people scattered, and doves flapped out of their cages. It was complete chaos.

   We might feel puzzled by this seemingly contradictory behavior of Jesus. After all, He did say, "I am gentle and humble in heart" (See Matthew 11:21). But here is the problem: Sometimes we equate meekness with weakness. A good definition of meekness is "power under constraint."

   Meekness is not weakness.

   Meekness is being able to do something, yet choosing not to.

   Weakness is not being able to do anything. Meekness is when the bully punches you, and you know you could take the bully out, but you decide that is not the best course of action. Weakness is not being able to hit back when the bully hits you.

I find it interesting that people usually are meek when it comes to defending others, but not themselves. In other words, they will rise up in anger when someone wrongs or hurts them, but they will say or do nothing when someone else is wronged.

Jesus was the very opposite of that. He was not angry in anticipation of the harm these people would do to him. In fact, he took the full brunt of their wrath when he allowed himself to be crucified. That was meekness—power under constraint. But he was indignant and angry when God's people were hurt and were prevented from worshiping.

The bottom line is that the merchants and religious leaders were keeping people away from God. And that made him angry. Very angry. God, even at this time, welcomed all people, both Jews and Gentiles.

God still welcomes all people. Therefore, the church should be open to all people. — Greg Laurie, *As I See It: Thoughts on Current Issues and Things That Matter from a Biblical Perspective* (Dana Point, CA: Kerygma Publishing—Allen David Books, 2011).

2. Why did Jesus denounce these cities? What had they done wrong? What is the lesson for us?

Jesus' harsh reproach against the cities in which most of His miracles were done seems on the surface to be less justified than His comparatively mild rebuke of those who openly criticized Him. For the most part, the three cities mentioned here-which typified all the places where His miracles were done-did not take any direct action against Jesus. They simply ignored Him. While the Son of God preached, taught, and performed unprecedented miracles in their midst, they carried on their business and their lives as usual, seemingly unaffected. From the human perspective, their indifference appears foolish but it does not appear to be terribly sinful. — John F. MacArthur Jr., *Matthew, MacArthur New Testament Commentary* (Chicago: Moody Press, 1985), Mt 11:20.

3. Why is ignoring Jesus such a heinous crime?

But indifference is a heinous form of unbelief. It so completely disregards God that He is not even an issue worth arguing about. He is not taken seriously enough to criticize.

As the young King Josiah declared, the great sin of Israel in that day was that the people had "not listened to the words of this book, to do according to all that is written concerning us." And for that disregard of God's Word the king said, "the wrath of the Lord … burns against us" (2 Kings 22:13).

In the parable of the royal wedding feast, the guests who were first invited "paid no attention and went their way, one to his own farm, another to his business" (Matt. 22:5). They did not mistreat and kill the king's slaves as some of the other citizens did (v. 6), but they were equally excluded from the feast. They picture the many people Christ calls but whose indifference excludes them from being among the few who are chosen (v. 14).

Indifference to the Lord will continue in the world until He returns. "Just as it happened in the days of Noah, so it shall be also in the days of the Son of Man," Jesus said; "they were eating, they were drinking, they were marrying, they were being given in marriage, until the day that Noah entered the ark, and the flood came and destroyed them all. It was the same as happened in the days of Lot: they were eating, they were drinking, they were buying, they were selling, they were planting, they were building; … It will be just the same on the day that the Son of Man is revealed" (Luke 17:26–28, 30). Some of the people in Noah's day doubtlessly criticized him abusively for building a ship in the middle of the desert; and some of the worst inhabitants of Sodom tried to homosexually attack the angels who came to rescue Lot. But most of the people in the days of Noah and of Lot paid no attention to the Lord or to His servants. Yet they, too, were totally destroyed, because they rejected God just as totally as those who actively expressed their unbelief.

Jesus' righteous anger boiled against the privileged cities who witnessed the awesome evidence of His divine power and goodness yet did not repent. In His holy fury He declared to them, Woe to you, Chorazin! Woe to you, Bethsaida! — John F. MacArthur Jr., *Matthew, MacArthur New Testament Commentary* (Chicago: Moody Press, 1985), Mt 11:20.

4. **Verse 21. How could Jesus know how Tyre and Sidon would have responded if they had received the gospel?**

How could anyone possibly know what might have happened under a certain set of circumstances if they had indeed come to pass? In fact, in our court system, if an attorney asks a "What if … ?" question to a witness, the witness's attorney will immediately object: "Calls for speculation!" And the objection will normally be sustained. Why? Because we can't possibly know what might happen under any given set of circumstances.

But God knows! He knows everything that has happened and everything that might have happened. We cannot even comprehend that kind of knowledge, of course. But that's the whole point: God is God and we're not. No wonder David wrote in Psalm 139:6, "Such knowledge is too wonderful for me; it is high, I cannot attain it."

Here is how God's omniscience impacts four areas of our spiritual life. — David Jeremiah, *Knowing the God You Worship: Study Guide* (Nashville, TN: Thomas Nelson Publishers, 2004), 81.

5. **Verse 24. Note the phrase, "more bearable." Does this suggest there will be some parts of Hell that are hotter than others? Are there degrees of punishment in Hell?**

The phrase "get off easier" is a revealing one. Not everyone will be judged by the same standard. The greater our privilege, the greater our responsibilities. Chorazin and Bethsaida saw much, so much was expected of them. The gospel was clearly presented to them, yet they clearly rejected it. "The saddest road to hell is that which runs under the pulpit, past the Bible and through the midst of warnings and invitations."

On the other hand, Tyre and Sidon saw less, so less was expected. They, to use the words of Christ, will "get off easier" than others. The principle? God's judgment is based upon humanity's response to the message received. He will never hold us accountable for what he doesn't tell us.

At the same time, he will never let us die without telling us something. Even those who never heard of Christ are given a message about the character of God. "The heavens declare the glory of God; the skies proclaim the work of his hands. Day after day they pour forth speech; night after night, they display knowledge. There is no speech or language where their voice is not heard" (Ps. 19:1–3 NIV).

Nature is God's first missionary. Where there is no Bible, there are sparkling stars. Where there are no preachers, there are springtimes. Where there is no testament of Scripture, there is the testament of changing seasons and breath-stealing sunsets. If a person has nothing but nature, then nature is enough to reveal something about God. As Paul says: "The basic reality of God is plain enough. Open your eyes and there it is! By taking a long and thoughtful look at what God has created, people have always been able to see what their eyes can't see: eternal power, for instance and the mystery of his divine being" (Rom. 1:20 MSG). — Max Lucado, *When Christ Comes: The Beginning of the Very Best* (Nashville, TN: Word Pub., 1999), 103–104.

6. **Verse 25. How literally do you take this? Does the Father hide the gospel from some and not from others?**

There is a deep unfathomable mystery here. Why does God hide the gospel from anyone, no matter how proud they are? Why doesn't he, through his providence, humble everyone? He humbled Nebuchadnezzar, why not a Donald Trump? He humbled Naaman, why not a Rush Limbaugh? Why not take all the Muhammad Alis of the world—"I am the greatest"— and show them, by whatever means, just how great they are not? I don't know. God's sovereign election is indeed a deep and unfathomable mystery to me. But I believe God's Word. And I know myself. I know that I was not so good that God should save me, be gracious to me, and open my heart as he did Lydia's (Acts 16:14). Why choose me from this rubble of humanity? And I know that God would be just in damning all and saving none, and thus is gracious (as v. 26 powerfully asserts) in saving some, revealing himself, revealing his Son to those who come to him for rest, who come to him in humility.

Why do some people come to Christ and others don't? One side of the coin is God's sovereignty: "I ... will show mercy on whom I will show mercy" (see Exodus 33:19; cf. Romans 9:15). The other side of the coin is human responsibility. Humility opens the door to the kingdom, and pride keeps it closed. And in 11:23, 25 the door-slamming sin of pride is addressed by our Lord. — Douglas Sean O'Donnell, *Matthew: All Authority in Heaven and on Earth, ed. R. Kent Hughes, Preaching the Word* (Wheaton, IL: Crossway, 2013), 302.

7. Verse 25. Who are the wise and learned? Who are the children?

Then, in 11:25, Jesus speaks of "the wise and understanding" versus "little children." "The wise and understanding" have the gospel "hidden" from them, while it is "revealed ... to little children." Here the contrast is not against the smart and the dumb or the adults and the kids, but rather between "those who are self-sufficient and deem themselves wise and those who are dependent and love to be taught."

It is the contrast in the Gospels between "the entire religious aristocracy" and the twelve ordinary men, between the Scriptural-savvy scribes and the seemingly gullible fishermen. It's the difference between the Pharisee who lifts his eyes to Heaven ("O Lord, I'm glad I'm not like them") and the tax collector who pounds his chest ("O Lord, have mercy upon me, a sinner") (see Luke 18:10–14). It's the difference between Caiaphas, who points at our Lord and demands in effect, "Are you the Son of God?" (cf. 26:63) and the Roman centurion who points to Christ crucified and says, "Truly this was the Son of God!" (27:54). It's the difference between the rich young ruler who walked away distraught, with his camel-sized pockets still heavy with gold, and little Zacchaeus, who climbed up a big sycamore tree and after he came down opened his heart to Jesus and his pockets to the poor. It's the difference between the proud in heart and the poor in spirit. It's the difference between conceited self-reliance and meek dependence upon God through Christ.

So, if you find yourself interested enough in the person of Christ, thinking, "Yes, this Jesus is quite the fellow. I'll admit that much," here's my advice to you: turn the lens you have on him back on yourself and ask, are you little enough in your own eyes to see him for who he is? You see, God is not looking for big shots. He is not interested in the somebodies of this world. He is interested in the nobodies (see 1 Corinthians 1:26–31). Are you enough of a nobody for him to be interested in you? That is, before him do you humbly confess your unworthiness, emptiness, and helplessness? Do you acknowledge that you are not good enough for God? Or has your education, wealth, power, position, talent, or knowledge puffed you up (cf. 1 Corinthians 8:1) and made you like a proud peacock, with your feathers spread too wide to walk through the narrow gate to freedom?

"God opposes the proud, but gives grace to the humble" (Proverbs 3:34 LXX; James 4:6; 1 Peter 5:5). "There are six things that the LORD hates, seven that are an abomination to him ... [number one!] haughty eyes" (Proverbs 6:16, 17). "Whoever exalts himself will be humbled, and whoever humbles himself will be exalted" (23:12). Do you want to become a son or daughter of the heavenly Father? You must become childlike in faith, trust, and dependence (cf. 18:3). You must become like a newborn; yes, you must become, as it were, born again. — Douglas Sean O'Donnell, *Matthew: All Authority in Heaven and on Earth, ed. R. Kent Hughes, Preaching the Word* (Wheaton, IL: Crossway, 2013), 302–303.

8. **Verse 28 mentions burdens. What are some burdens that people today—in this church—carry?**

When Jesus says, "Come to me, all you who are weary and burdened," even the happiest man, woman, or child here is thankful for the offer. For we all bear burdens. Consider some of the burdens we bear:

- We visit a couple we love and grieve when they speak most unkindly to each other. We worry about their marriage; we are burdened for our friends.

- We learn that a friend or mentor in a distant place has cancer. He may not live to the end of the year.

- We have a new job, helping a company improve its product. We thought we could help, and we certainly have the ability, but there are obstacles in the workplace that thwart every effort to turn things around.

- For some reason you cannot seem to get a good night's sleep. You wake up every morning burdened by near exhaustion.

Jesus bids us to come to him, that he may bear our burdens and give us rest. It is one of the sweetest promises of Scripture, but to understand it we first must see that Jesus bears a burden—a burden he explains in Matthew 11:25–30. — Daniel M. Doriani, *Matthew & 2, ed. Richard D. Phillips, Philip Graham Ryken, and Daniel M. Doriani, vol. 1, Reformed Expository Commentary* (Phillipsburg, NJ: P&R Publishing, 2008), 478–479.

9. **Matthew 11.28 – 30. What do we learn about Jesus from this classic passage? What do we learn about following Jesus?**

Farmers in ancient Israel used to train an inexperienced ox by yoking it to an experienced one with a wooden harness. The straps around the older animal were tightly drawn. He carried the load. But the yoke around the younger animal was loose.

He walked alongside the more mature ox, but his burden was light. In this verse Jesus is saying, "I walk alongside you. We are yoked together. But I pull the weight and carry the burden."

I wonder, how many burdens is Jesus carrying for us that we know nothing about? We're aware of some. He carries our sin. He carries our shame. He carries our eternal debt. But are there others? Has he lifted fears before we felt them? Has he carried our confusion so we wouldn't have to? Those times when we have been surprised by our own sense of peace? Could it be that Jesus has lifted our anxiety onto his shoulders and placed a yoke of kindness on ours? — Max Lucado, *A Love Worth Giving : Living in the Overflow of God's Love* (Nashville, Tenn.: W Pub. Group, 2002).

10. Who is Jesus addressing in this passage? Who does He have in mind as He speaks?

The tense in the first verb of the phrase, weary and burdened, conveys the idea of continual weariness and exhaustion, without a minute of relief. The perfect tense in the second verb implies that the people were completely loaded up at some time in the past, and the load remains perpetually on them. These people needed a break! Pharisaical legalism surrounding the Mosaic Law had ground them to spiritual powder. The Lord offered himself to them. — Stuart K. Weber, *Matthew, vol. 1, Holman New Testament Commentary* (Nashville, TN: Broadman & Holman Publishers, 2000), 169.

11. Is Christian living easy or hard?

The Christian life is either easy or impossible. It is either a day-to-day struggle that you are no doubt losing, or it is a delightful paradise of buoyant emotion. It either pulls you up with tremendous power to overcome all kinds of obstacles and circumstances, or it is a very heavy load. Jesus taught that if it is a heavy load, you purchased the wrong product: "For my yoke is easy and my burden is light." (Matthew 11:30). If Christianity is very heavy for you, this book is for you. I have written it with the hope that it will result in making your burden lighter.

The Puritans wisely wrote:

> The chief end of man is to glorify God and enjoy him forever.

C.S. Lewis wrote in a letter to a friend:

> It is a Christian duty, as you know, for everyone to be as happy as he can.

David said it this way:

> "Delight yourself in the LORD and he will give you the desires of your heart." Psalms 37:4

And Paul thought this concept so important he had to repeat himself:

> Finally, my brothers, rejoice in the Lord! It is no trouble for me to write the same things to you again, and it is a safeguard for you. Philippians 3:1

> Rejoice in the Lord always. I will say it again: Rejoice! Philippians 4:4

Jesus taught that if it is a heavy load, you purchased the wrong product: "For my yoke is easy and my burden is light." — Josh Hunt, *People Who Enjoy Their God*, 2012.

12. Based on this verse, what advice would you have for a friend who said that Christian living was very, very hard?

Following God's plan made his load lighter. Have you ever considered that following God's plan for your life might make your schedule easier? Moses load became lighter by following God's plan, "That will make your load lighter." (Exodus 18:22) In a similar way, Jesus said, "My yoke is easy and my burden is light." (Matthew 11:30) If the ministry is not easy for you, you might look to see whose yoke you are pulling. Christian ministry ought to become lighter and lighter as we learn to do it better and better. If the work of the ministry is not becoming easier for you, reevaluate what you are doing.

Many plans have trade-offs; some things are better while certain others are worse. Not so delegation. Jethro taught Moses that as he followed God's plan it would be good for the people as well as for Moses. "If you do this and God so commands, you will be able to stand the strain, and all these people will go home satisfied." (Exodus 18:23) Delegation benefits everyone: the leader who delegates, the people he delegates to, and the people who receive the ministry. Everyone is a winner. — Josh Hunt, *You Can Double Your Class in Two Years or Less*, 1995.

13. What is a yoke? What does a yoke do?

In that agrarian culture, everyone knew that a yoke (11:29, 30) went across the necks of two beasts of burden, just in front of their shoulders, and connected them to the plow or wagon they were to pull. Under the covenant relationship, the believer is not relieved of all work or burden, but is given work that is appropriate to his abilities, within his limitations. In fact, the believer will find the work fulfilling and rewarding rather than toilsome and exhausting. Jesus' yoke is easy (suitable, good, reasonable), and his burden is light (easy to bear, insignificant).

Jesus instructed his followers to take my yoke at their own initiative. Jesus will not put it on us without our consent. But to refuse Jesus' yoke is not to be burden-free, but to retain a much heavier burden. Everyone in life must carry a burden; the question is whether we will carry one that is within our capacity, or one heavier than we were designed for. — Stuart K. Weber, *Matthew, vol. 1, Holman New Testament Commentary* (Nashville, TN: Broadman & Holman Publishers, 2000), 169.

14. Do you ever feel tired? What message does this passage have for the tired?

Although it took place in the 1930s, it remains one of the most mystifying missing person cases in FBI files. After spending an evening eating out with friends, a forty-five-year-old New York judge hailed a taxi and was never seen or heard from again. The FBI immediately became involved. They suspected a kidnapping by someone who held a judicial grudge against him. But that didn't seem to pan out. They then suspected Mafia activity because he was an outspoken enemy of the Mafia. But again, that led nowhere. To this day, there is only one clue that remains. When his wife returned to their apartment the evening her husband disappeared, there on the table was a check for a large sum of money made out to her and a note attached to it in her husband's handwriting which simply said,

I am very, very tired. Love, Joe

The question remains—were those words merely a comment made at the end of a particularly trying day? Or was his note saying, "I'm tired; I'm fatigued; I'm weary; I give up"? To this day, we can't be sure. For lack of further evidence, it is presently believed he rode off in a taxicab to an unknown destination where he took his own life because weariness had weighted his soul. I think all of us from time to time can relate to that kind of weariness. I'm not speaking of physical fatigue—the kind of fatigue you feel after mowing the lawn or playing a set of tennis. No, I'm speaking of the weariness which comes from life itself. — Jon Courson, *Jon Courson's Application Commentary* (Nashville, TN: Thomas Nelson, 2003), 81.

15. What do we learn about being Christlike from this passage?

As bold as those claims appear, Jesus also described Himself as "gentle" and "humble of heart." Jesus spoke Aramaic, but Matthew recorded his story in Greek. In doing so, he chose two terms to convey Jesus' original thoughts.

The first is praus, which generally meant "mild," "friendly," or "pleasant," but readers of the Old Testament would know the verb as "to find oneself in a stunted, humble, lowly position." It was a social and economic term for "'one who is in the position of a servant.' It describes the man who has no property and who has thus to earn his bread by serving others."4 Old Testament prophets later picked up the term to describe those who were obedient to God and who bore their exile from the Promised Land with a quiet, hopeful trust in the Lord without a hint of anger. In other words, it describes a person who has absolutely no sense of entitlement.

Jesus said of the Pharisees, "They do all their deeds to be noticed by men; for they broaden their phylacteries and lengthen the tassels of their garments. They love the place of honor at banquets and the chief seats in the synagogues, and respectful greetings in the market places, and being called Rabbi by men" (Matthew 23:5–7).

The second, tapeinos, pictures someone bowing low and thus means "bowed down," "small," "insignificant in comparison to something else." In the Old Testament, it describes the posture of a righteous person before God. — Charles R. Swindoll, *Jesus: The Greatest Life of All* (Nashville: Thomas Nelson, 2011).

16. What does rest represent in this passage?

Rest for the soul: Such was the first promise extended by the Savior to win the burdened sinner. Simple though it appears, the promise is as large and comprehensive as can be found. Rest for the soul—does it not imply deliverance from every fear, the supply of every want, the fulfillment of every desire? And now this is the prize with which the Savior woos back the wandering one, the one who is mourning that his rest has not been so abiding or so full as he had hoped, to return and abide in Him. This was the reason that rest either has not been found, or, if found, has been disturbed or lost again: you did not abide in Him.

Have you ever noticed how, in the original invitation of the Savior to come to Him (Matthew 11:28–29), the promise of rest was repeated twice, with such a variation in the conditions as might suggest that abiding rest can only be found in abiding nearness. First the Savior says, "Come to Me, and I will give you rest"; the very moment you come, and believe, I will give you rest, the rest of pardon and acceptance found in my love. But we know that all that God bestows needs time to become fully our own. It must be embraced, appropriated, and assimilated into our soul; without this not even Christ's giving can make it our own in terms of full experience and enjoyment.

And so the Savior repeats His promise, in words that clearly speak not so much of the initial rest with which He welcomes the weary one who comes, but of the deeper and personally appropriated rest of the soul that abides in Him. Now He not only says "Come to Me" but also "Take My yoke upon you and learn from Me"; become My scholars, yield yourselves to My training, submit in all things to My will, let your whole life be one with mine—in other words, abide in Me. And then He adds not only "I will give" but also "you will find rest for your souls." The rest that He gave at your first coming will become something you have really found and made your very own—the deeper, abiding rest which comes from longer acquaintance, closer fellowship, and entire surrender. "Take My yoke, and learn from Me," "Abide in Me"—this is the path to abiding rest. — Andrew Murray, *Abiding in Christ* (Grand Rapids, MI: Bethany House, 2003).

17. Hebrews 4 uses rest as a picture of Christian living. In what way is Christian living like rest?

Matthew 11:28-30 contains a beautiful description of the purpose and pace of the Spirit-filled walk. Jesus invites you to a restful walk in tandem with Him, just as two oxen walk together under the same yoke. "How can a yoke be restful?" you ask. Because Jesus' yoke is an easy yoke. As the lead ox, Jesus walks at a steady pace. If you pace yourself with Him, your burden will be easy. But if you take a passive approach to the relationship, you'll be painfully dragged along in the yoke because Jesus keeps walking. Or if you try to race ahead or turn off in another direction, the yoke will chafe your neck and your life will be uncomfortable. The key to a restful yoke-relationship with Jesus is to learn from Him and open yourself to His gentleness and humility.

The picture of walking in the Spirit in tandem with Jesus also helps us understand our service to God. How much will you get done without Jesus pulling on His side of the yoke? Nothing. And how much will be accomplished without you on your side? Nothing. A yoke can only work if both are pulling together.

Paul said, "I planted, Apollos watered, but God was causing the growth" (1 Corinthians 3:6). You and I have the privilege to plant and water, but if God isn't in it, nothing will grow. However, if we don't plant and water, nothing will grow. God has chosen to work through the church, in partnership with you to do His work in the world today. He's the lead ox. Let's learn from Him. — Neil T. Anderson and Joanne Anderson, *Daily in Christ* (Eugene, OR: Harvest House, 2000).

18. How would you turn this passage into a prayer?

We are strangers to many things, our Father, but most of all to silence. We find ourselves so busily engaged in life that we hate to miss even one panel of a revolving door. We dash to work ... we rush through the day ... we choke down our lunch ... we speed through each afternoon ... and we hurry home. Our activity is constant. Rarely—if ever—do we deliberately slow down ... sit in silence ... and let the wonder in. Help us to do that right now. May we rest in You in the quietness of this moment. May we be still and learn anew that You are God.

We cast our cares on You. We release our struggles and place them on Your shoulders. We give our worried hearts to You. We rest in knowing You command a multitude of capable angels to watch over us, Your children, because You love us. We rest in the knowledge that Your Spirit empowers us to live a life that is beyond our own ability. Our victory reflects Your power, not ours. That strips away all the pride, all the strain, all the self-effort. You free us to rest in the joy of who You are. We thank You for all these things in the name of Jesus, who is our rest. Amen. — Charles, *Hear Me When I*

Call: Learning to Connect with a God Who Cares (Brentwood, TN: Worthy Publishing, 2013).

19. What do you want to recall from today's conversation?

20. How can we support one another in prayer this week?

Sentence prayers. As discussed in the previous chapter, praying aloud in a group is very difficult for some people. To make it a bit easier, try one-sentence prayers. Tell group members, "We are going to go around the room and offer God one-sentence prayers. No longer. It can be as simple as 'Thank you' or a bit longer. But remember, keep it to one sentence." Not only does this make it easier for reluctant group members to offer a simple prayer, but it also keeps the more verbose members from monopolizing prayer time.

Pray in trios. During prayer time, break into groups of three and spend a bit more time sharing your prayer requests with each other. Before returning to the rest of the group, be sure to take turns praying for each individual in your group of three.

I love this church! As a group, make a list of things you love about your church. Then spend some time thanking God for bringing you to such a church. Then ask group members: "What one thing could we do to make our church even better?" Once you come up with an answer, decide how your group can make that happen.

Traits of God. Bring a poster board to the group meeting and ask members to brainstorm and come up with character traits of God (forgiving, loving, and so forth). After you have listed all of the traits you can think of, spend some time in prayer and thanksgiving for these traits.

A night of worship. Ask group members to bring their favorite worship song (on CD or DVD) to the next group meeting. During that meeting, play each person's song and ask the person to share what that song means to him or her.

Set the mood. Treat your group prayer time as something special—which it is! Spend a moment to dim the lighting, light some candles, or play quiet instrumental music in the background. This can be a great way to focus members and remind them of the importance of prayer. — Steve Gladen, *Leading Small Groups with Purpose: Everything You Need to Lead a Healthy Group* (Grand Rapids, MI: Baker, 2012).

Lesson #12, Matthew 12.38 - 42
Good Questions Have Groups Talking
www.joshhunt.com

Matthew 12.38 - 42

OPEN

Let's each share your name and, and one thing that makes you mad

DIG

1. **Look at the context. What do you think the Pharisees are feeling as they approach Jesus?**

   The Pharisees must have been smarting from their verbal defeat by Jesus. Jesus had shown that their evil explanation of his miracles—that he was casting out demons by the power of Satan—was both absurd and contradictory. His arguments should have moved them to reconsider their position, but they did not, of course. They hated Jesus, so rather than altering their views, they merely came at him from another direction, demanding a miraculous sign. — James Montgomery Boice, *The Gospel of Matthew* (Grand Rapids, MI: Baker Books, 2001), 218–220.

2. **Does Jesus' response seems somewhat harsh? Why do you think Jesus is being a bit harsh in His response?**

   Would miracles make more people believe? Would unbelievers become believers if they were to see a bona fide miracle? The scribes and Pharisees' demand for a sign prompted Jesus to give them some of His most solemn and searching words:

"An evil and adulterous generation seeks after a sign, and no sign will be given to it except the sign of the prophet Jonah. ... The men of Ninevah will rise in the judgment with this generation and condemn it, because they repented at the preaching of Jonah; and indeed a greater than Jonah is here." (Matthew 12:39, 41)

A casual reading of Jesus' response seems almost harsh. After all, here were some individuals who were simply asking for a miracle. He had performed many of them. What's one more? Perhaps that miracle could have brought them to faith. Why didn't He grant their request?

The answer is that Jesus always looks at the motives behind what people say and do. He is far more interested in what is going on in our hearts than what is coming out of our mouths. As He looked in their hearts, no doubt He saw the real reason behind their request: They wanted to destroy Jesus. Matthew 12:14 tells us that the Pharisees "took counsel against Him, how they might destroy Him."

Jesus died on the cross for them and for all of humanity, and rose again from the dead, because we all were separated from God by sin. That is the message Jesus essentially was giving to the Pharisees. That is the message He essentially is giving to us. It is the greatest sign of all. It is the ultimate sign. — Greg Laurie, *For Every Season: Daily Devotions* (Dana Point, CA: Kerygma Publishing—Allen David Books, 2011).

3. What was the Pharisees's motive in asking for a sign?

So what was the motive of these Pharisees. They wanted to destroy Jesus. They weren't interested in a miracle. They weren't interested in a sign. They were out to get Him. And Jesus recognized this. — Greg Laurie, *The Greg Laurie Sermon Archive* (Riverside, CA: Harvest Ministries, 2014).

4. What sign could Jesus have done to convince the Pharisees?

A sign? Whatever were they thinking? Some scholars try to explain their demand by suggesting that they were asking for a different kind of sign from those Jesus had already given, a sign produced on demand perhaps. But what sign could Jesus have given in addition to the miracles he had done? He told the disciples of John the Baptist, "Go back and report to John what you hear and see: The blind receive sight, the lame walk, those who have leprosy are cured, the deaf hear, the dead are raised, and the good news is preached to the poor" (Matt. 11:4–5). These were true messianic signs, and Jesus had performed them, which means that in light of his miracles the demand for a "sign" was both insulting and impudent. It was also hypocritical, for regardless of what Jesus might have done to meet their demand, these men would merely have dug their heels in deeper and refused to believe him. — James Montgomery Boice, *The Gospel of Matthew* (Grand Rapids, MI: Baker Books, 2001), 220.

5. Do you think the Pharisees wanted to believe? Do you think they wanted it to be true that Jesus was the Son of God?

The rebel is not simply someone who doesn't believe. He or she is someone who doesn't want to believe. Rebels do not want the story of Jesus to be true. They do not want to live in the universe governed by the kind of Father whom Jesus himself trusted and described. And this desire goes so deep that it colors the way they look at every argument and every bit of evidence and makes sure they find a way not to believe.

Rebels are afraid of what would happen if they were to surrender themselves to God. So they just defy. Skeptics abstain because they don't know who to vote for. Cynics abstain because they are suspicious of everybody. Rebels don't just abstain; they secede to set up their own little dictatorship. Skeptics question, cynics suspect, rebels defy.

Edward Ruffin was a rebel of the Confederacy. He fired the first shot of the Civil War at Fort Sumter then fought the

Yankees for four years. He lost his plantation and fortune along the way. When the war was over, the South had lost, and the slaves were free, he wrote a note on June 17, 1865, declaring his "unmitigated hatred to Yankee rule . . . and for the perfidious, malignant, and vile Yankee race." Then he blew out his brains.

C. S. Lewis said that when he was an unbeliever, atheism was not only his belief, it was his strongest desire. "No word in my vocabulary expressed deeper hatred than the word interference." And he was uncomfortably aware that the Hebrew and Christian Scriptures "placed at the center what seemed to be a transcendental Interferer." Atheism appealed to his deep desire to be left alone. Rebels fear being interfered with. — John Ortberg, *Know Doubt: Embracing Uncertainty in Your Faith* (Grand Rapids, MI: Zondervan, 2014).

6. Think about unbelievers you know. Do you think they want to believe? Do you think they want the gospel to be true? Are they looking for answers?

"What do I want to believe?" is one of the most important questions we can ask when it comes to the search for faith.

It is crucial to be honest about this, because over time we have a tendency to find ourselves believing what we want to believe. Remember, Bart called himself a "cheerful" agnostic. Philosopher Thomas Nagel wrote, "I want atheism to be true. It isn't just that I don't believe in God. I don't want there to be a God. I don't want the universe to be like that."

Maybe Marx was right — faith is the opium of the people, exploited by the elite to stay in power. Maybe some people have a "god gene" that predisposes them to believe just as others are genetically predisposed to become alcoholics or left-handers or yodelers. Maybe Freud was right and "the religions of mankind must be classed among the mass delusions . . . the universal obsessional neurosis of humanity." Freud proposed in Totem and Taboo that both religious faith and guilt arose when a primal horde of men grew jealous of their father — a despot who had seized all the women for himself — and therefore killed him, ate his body, and then instituted the ritual sacrifice of an animal ("totem") as a way to displace their guilt. Belief in God is just a giant oedipal projection of our wishes upon the cosmos. Freud actually seriously argued that religion started because an early tribe of men killed the father and felt guilty about it and invented religion to deal with their guilt and make sure it wouldn't get repeated. This particular idea of his has not caught on widely.

Karl Marx's drug analogy can cut both ways. Nobel laureate Czeslaw Milosz observed in The Discreet Charm of Nihilism, "A true opium of the people is the belief of nothingness after death — a huge solace for thinking that we are not going to be judged for our betrayals, greed, cowardice, murders." — John Ortberg, *Know Doubt: Embracing Uncertainty in Your Faith* (Grand Rapids, MI: Zondervan, 2014).

7. Why would anyone not want to believe there is a God?

Sometimes the existence of God would turn out to be — borrowing a phrase from former U.S. Vice President Al Gore — "an inconvenient truth." I liked Denny, but I couldn't figure out why he kept wanting to meet. He was a large man, a construction guy, and I was a little intimidated. He wanted to talk about God, so we did, and he asked one difficult question after another about faith — one tough intellectual issue after another. We would talk each one through to as much resolution as we could get, and he would always bring up another one. Finally, I asked him, "If all of these issues were settled, if every intellectual barrier you raised were dismantled, is there anything else besides all this intellectual stuff that would hold you back from following Jesus?"

There was a long silence. Denny did not like the question. It turned out that he was involved in sexual behavior that he knew was not honoring to God and that, if he were to become a follower of Jesus, would have to change. He didn't want to change. His mind caused him to find all kinds of objections, but the reality was that he did not want it to be true. He was afraid of what he would have to do if it were.

If Denny had been smaller, I probably would have pointed this out earlier. — John Ortberg, *Know Doubt: Embracing Uncertainty in Your Faith* (Grand Rapids, MI: Zondervan, 2014).

8. Is this saying it is wrong to look for, or feel the need for evidence to bolster our faith?

Becoming a Christian requires a leap of faith but not a blind leap. Anyone who receives Jesus does so by faith, but this faith rests on a mountain of evidence.

We were not there to see the resurrection with our own eyes, but the New Testament records many compelling accounts from those who were, not to mention repeated passages from the Old Testament (such as Isa. 53 and Ps. 22, written centuries beforehand) that so precisely detail the crucifixion and resurrection that it's hard to explain them away. Many of the early disciples suffered brutal deaths rather than deny their assertion that Jesus had risen from the grave and had spoken with them repeatedly. And how do we explain the conversion of the once rabidly anti-Christian Saul of Tarsus, who repeatedly stated that the resurrected Jesus had personally appointed him an apostle? — *Walk Thru The Bible, Stand Firm Day by Day: Let Nothing Move You* (Nashville: B&H, 2013).

9. Would you say ours is a reasonable faith?

Many people suspect that putting their faith in Christ involves shutting down their brain and making a blind, emotional leap of faith in denial of everything that their rational mind would have told them had they not chosen to turn it off. Not so.

The Christian faith is based on truth. God exists. Christianity is based on actual historical facts. It is reasonable and true. It can stand the scrutiny of rational minds and bring even scholars and scientists to their knees. — Ed Strauss, *One Hundred and Fifty Need-to-Know Bible Facts: Key Truths for Better Living* (Uhrichsville, OH: Barbour, 2011).

10. What evidence convinced you of the truthfulness of the claims of the Bible?

Some philosophy can help establish the truth of Christianity. For example, here are some philosophical arguments for the existence of God:

The cosmological argument. Every effect must have an adequate cause. The universe is an effect. Reason demands that whatever caused the universe must be greater than the universe. That cause is God—who Himself is the uncaused First Cause (Hebrews 3:4).

The teleological argument. The universe displays an obvious purposeful design. This perfect design argues for a Designer, and that Designer is God (Psalm 19:1-4).

The moral argument. Every human being has an innate sense of "oughtness," or moral obligation. Where did this sense of oughtness come from? It must come from God. The existence of a moral law in our hearts demands the existence of a moral Lawgiver (Romans 1:19-32).

The anthropological argument. Human beings have a personality (mind, emotions, and will). Since the personal cannot come from the impersonal, there must be a personal cause—and that personal cause is God (Genesis 1:26-27).

The ontological argument. Most human beings have an innate idea of a perfect being. Where did this idea come from? Not from man, for man is an imperfect being. Some perfect being must have planted the idea there. Thus God must in fact exist. — Ron Rhodes, *5-Minute Apologetics for Today: 365 Quick Answers to Key Questions* (Eugene, OR: Harvest House, 2010).

11. Have you read any books on apologetics? What books would you recommend to someone who wanted more information to bolster their faith?

Know Doubt, Ortberg
I Don't Have Enough Faith to Be an Atheist, Geisler
Mere Christianity, Lewis

12. Jesus accused the Pharisees of being wicked and sinful. Did they look wicked and sinful? What is the lesson for us?

Although truly righteous people will manifest the godly evidence of that righteousness, some people appear to be righteous who are not, because man's basic sinfulness is not most fully revealed by what he does or says-despite the importance of those evidences, as Jesus has just made clear (vv. 33–37). Sin is most clearly and indisputably manifested by how a person responds to Jesus Christ. No matter what a person's outward life is like, his innate spiritual nature and his true attitude toward God are seen with absolute certainty in his attitude toward Jesus Christ. The person who rejects Christ is dead spiritually and an enemy of God, no matter what religious profession he may make or how morally and selflessly he may appear to live. The issue of sin becomes perfectly focused when a person confronts Christ, and the crux of damning sin is rejection of Him. Men are convicted of "sin because they do not believe in Me," Jesus said (John 16:9). — John F. MacArthur Jr., *Matthew, MacArthur New Testament Commentary* (Chicago: Moody Press, 1985), Mt 12:38.

13. What do we learn about being Christlike from Jesus' behavior in this passage?

You may have certain pictures of Jesus hanging in the gallery of your mind. Meek and mild may be one of them—and it is certainly an appropriate picture. It should not be the only one, how-ever. You need to picture Jesus as the coming King of kings, who will one day ride to victory over all evil.

Then I saw heaven opened, and there before me was a white horse. The rider on the horse is called Faithful and True, and he is right when he judges and makes war. His eyes are like burning fire, and on his head are many crowns. . . . Out of the rider's mouth comes a sharp sword that he will use to defeat the nations, and he will rule them with a rod of iron. He will crush out the wine in the wine press of the terrible anger of God the Almighty. On his robe and on his upper leg was written this name: KINGOF KINGS AND LORD OF LORDS. (Revelation 19:11-16 NCV)

That is Jesus. He is indeed a Mighty Warrior, not just someday off in the future, but today, on your behalf. A battle is raging and you're right in the middle of it. You need a Mighty Warrior to fight with you. — Dee Brestin et al., *Jesus* (Nashville: Thomas Nelson, 2004).

14. Does this suggest we ought to confront every sin we see? When should we confront and when should keep our mouths shut?

- When someone is in danger. Some people say or do things that hurt themselves or others to the extent that lives are at risk. God opposes all abusive behavior whether it is self-inflicted or inflicted onto others. You need to intervene when you see any behavior that puts people in harm's way.

  "Rescue those being led away to death; hold back those staggering toward slaughter. If you say, 'But we knew nothing about this,' does not he who weighs the heart perceive it? Does not he who guards your life know it? Will he not repay each person according to what he has done?" (Proverbs 24:11–12)

- When a relationship is threatened. Relationships are vulnerable to damaging words or actions. You need to confront when necessary to preserve the relationship.

  "I plead with Euodia and I plead with Syntyche to agree with each other in the Lord. Yes, and I ask you, loyal yokefellow, help these women who have contended at my side in the cause of the gospel, along with Clement and the rest of my fellow workers, whose names are in the book of life." (Philippians 4:2–3)

- When division exists within a group. One of the enemy's tactics is to cause quarrels, strife, and jealousy among a body of believers. God calls us to unity, agreement, and peace. He charges us to guard and protect these precious relationships.

  "Let us therefore make every effort to do what leads to peace and to mutual edification." (Romans 14:19)

- When someone sins against you. Difficult though it may be, God gives you a clear directive to confront anyone who does something to you that clearly violates God's will in regard to how you are to be treated.

  "If your brother sins against you, go and show him his fault, just between the two of you. If he listens to you, you have won your brother over." (Matthew 18:15)

- When you are offended. Sometimes you can be offended by someone's actions even when the actions are not sinful. For the sake of the relationship, confronting in humility and exposing your concern allows the other person to be sensitive to you in the future and to not intentionally offend you by continuing the offensive actions.

  "Be completely humble and gentle; be patient, bearing with one another in love. Make every effort to keep the unity of the Spirit through the bond of peace." (Ephesians 4:2–3)

- When someone is caught in a sin. At times you will see a sin in others to which they are blind. While guarding against the possibility of the same sin in your own life, God wants to use you to expose the sin and help the one trapped to overcome it.

"When I [God] say to a wicked man, 'You will surely die,' and you do not warn him or speak out to dissuade him from his evil ways in order to save his life, that wicked man will die for his sin, and I will hold you accountable for his blood." (Ezekiel 3:18)

- When others are offended. Sometimes confronting on behalf of others is appropriate. In cases of prejudice, injustice, or violence toward those unable to defend themselves, God expects you to take up their cause and speak out against the wrong done to them. The apostle Paul confronted Peter openly,

"I opposed him to his face, because he was clearly in the wrong. Before certain men came from James, he used to eat with the Gentiles. But when they [the Jews] arrived, he began to draw back and separate himself from the Gentiles because he was afraid of those who belonged to the circumcision group. The other Jews joined him in his hypocrisy, so that by their hypocrisy even Barnabas was led astray." (Galatians 2:11–13) — June Hunt, *Biblical Counseling Keys on Confrontation: Challenging Others to Change* (Dallas, TX: Hope For The Heart, 2008), 10–11.

15. "Why can't I just forgive and forget? Why do I have to confront someone when they offend me?"

ANSWER: Undisclosed forgiveness benefits you by keeping you from becoming bitter, but it does not necessarily benefit your offender who is in need of correction. Yes, you need to forgive and not dwell on the offense, but you also need to confront in order to make your offender aware of a problem area that needs to be addressed. Forgiving without confronting can later result in your offender's resenting you for not caring enough to make the offense known so that the bad behavior could be changed. Your offender could then develop a bitter root that later bears bitter fruit.

"See to it that no one misses the grace of God and that no bitter root grows up to cause trouble and defile many." (Hebrews 12:15) — June Hunt, *Biblical Counseling Keys on*

Confrontation: Challenging Others to Change (Dallas, TX: Hope For The Heart, 2008), 11.

16. When should we *not* confront?

While confrontation can create unity, it can also divide. To avoid needless damage, you should not confront …

#1   When you are not the right person to confront. If you are not the one offended or not responsible for the one offended, you may not be the one who should confront. However, God might use you to help the person who is responsible to confront.

"Like one who seizes a dog by the ears is a passer-by who meddles in a quarrel not his own." (Proverbs 26:17)

#2   When it's not the right time to confront. You may be the right person to do the confronting, but it may not be the right time or your heart may not be right.

"There is a time for everything … a time to be silent and a time to speak." (Ecclesiastes 3:1, 7)

#3   When you are uncertain of the facts. Be sure you are fully informed of what is happening. Sometimes asking the right questions and listening objectively will reveal that you are simply misperceiving the situation.

"He who answers before listening—that is his folly and his shame." (Proverbs 18:13)

#4   When it's best to overlook a minor offense. You may find that overlooking minor offenses allows God to convict others of their errors. When in doubt, erring on the side of restraint and mercy is generally best.

"Hatred stirs up dissension, but love covers over all wrongs." (Proverbs 10:12)

#5   When you are committing the same sin. Paradoxically, you can be most offended by people who are engaging in the very behaviors with which you yourself struggle. We are hypocritical if we try to correct others when we ourselves are guilty of the same thing. First correct your own behavior. Then you can help correct the behavior of someone else.

"Why do you look at the speck of sawdust in your brother's eye and pay no attention to the plank in your own eye? How can you say to your brother, 'Let me take the speck out of your eye,' when all the time there is a plank in your own eye? You hypocrite, first take the plank out of your own eye, and then you will see clearly to remove the speck from your brother's eye." (Matthew 7:3–5)

#6   When your motive is purely your own rights, not the benefit of the other person. A "my rights" attitude will only damage the spirit of a positive confrontation. Therefore, consider another's interests over your own.

"Do nothing out of selfish ambition or vain conceit, but in humility consider others better than yourselves. Each of you should look not only to your own interests, but also to the interests of others." (Philippians 2:3–4)

#7   When you have a vindictive motive. Before you confront, genuine forgiveness of the offender is imperative. In your heart, release the offender into the hands of God. Your confrontation must not be to satisfy your secret desire to take revenge or to get even.

"Do not repay anyone evil for evil. Be careful to do what is right in the eyes of everybody." (Romans 12:17)

#8   When the consequences of the confrontation outweigh those of the offense. Look at the degree of the offense before you confront. Some battles pay little dividends and are just not worth the fight!

"Better a dry crust with peace and quiet than a house full of feasting, with strife." (Proverbs 17:1)

#9   When the person you want to confront has a habit of foolishness and quarreling. Avoid confronting people who are unwilling to recognize their offense. If you cannot avoid the confrontation, you may need to take others with you to help in confronting these persons.

"Don't have anything to do with foolish and stupid arguments, because you know they produce quarrels. And the Lord's servant must not quarrel; instead, he must be kind to everyone, able to teach, not resentful." (2 Timothy 2:23–24)

#10   When setting aside your rights will benefit an unbeliever. Jesus modeled suffering for righteousness' sake and exhorts you to endure unjust hardship for the sake of exposing God's character to the unbeliever. Allow room for God to work in another's heart by showing restraint.

"It is commendable if a man bears up under the pain of unjust suffering because he is conscious of God.… To this you were called, because Christ suffered for you, leaving you an example, that you should follow in his steps." (1 Peter 2:19, 21)

#11   When the person who offended you is your enemy. Sometimes it is best not to confront but to win them over by praying for them and blessing them. You and your offender are ultimately responsible to God for your actions. The path to peace might mean forgiving and blessing your offender without ever confronting the offensive behavior.

"Love your enemies and pray for those who persecute you, that you may be sons of your Father in heaven. He causes his sun to rise on the evil and the good, and sends rain on the righteous and the unrighteous." (Matthew 5:44–45)

#12   When confrontation will be ineffective and reprisal severe. You may not be able to effectively confront a person who has a violent temper and who is likely to exact severe retribution on you or on someone you love. (However, with such a person you still need to have and enforce proper boundaries.)

"Whoever corrects a mocker invites insult; whoever rebukes a wicked man incurs abuse." (Proverbs 9:7)

June Hunt, *Biblical Counseling Keys on Confrontation: Challenging Others to Change* (Dallas, TX: Hope For The Heart, 2008), 12–13.

17. Jesus compared Himself to Jonah. What did Jesus and Jonah have in common? How were they different?

"The one sign I will give you is the sign of Jonah. Jonah preached judgment. I have come preaching grace and mercy. Jonah was disobedient. I have come obediently. Jonah preached to one city. I have come for the whole world. A greater Prophet than Jonah is in your midst, yet you do not respond." — Jon Courson, *Jon Courson's Application Commentary* (Nashville, TN: Thomas Nelson, 2003), 91.

18. Verse 40. Jesus wasn't technically dead three days and three nights. How do you explain this?

don't get bogged down by the mathematics of verse 40, where Jesus speaks of the three days and three nights. Perhaps when you read that you might think, "Wait, wasn't Jesus buried for just one and a half days? He died at 'the ninth hour' (3:00 p.m.) on Friday, and then he was buried later that evening. So he was in the tomb some of Friday, all of Saturday, and then part of Sunday. That is not three days and nights."

The key to understanding the potential discrepancy of days here is first of all to understand how ancient Jews calculated time. A new day began after sunset (not at midnight), and part of a day was often counted as a whole day. I can give you five different examples from the Bible where this was the case. Matthew obviously knew the time line. Read the end of his Gospel. He knows how long Jesus was actually in the tomb. But to him and to his first readers, the count goes like this: Jesus was in the tomb—Friday, Saturday, and Sunday—one, two, three.6

However, this explanation does not explain the "three nights." This explains "three days" fine, but it does not explain the "three nights" part. Even if you count a new day beginning at sunset and a partial day as a whole day, Friday afternoon to Sunday morning does not make three nights. Perhaps then it is best to follow Vincent Taylor's understanding that the three days and nights means "in the shortest possible time."

Whatever the best clarification, let's please understand that the main idea here is not precision of time but similarity of sign: as Jonah went down and came up, so Jesus will die and rise again. So, yes, there is a time correlation, but more so a sign relation. And the whole point of verses 39, 40 is that only one sign will be given to that generation, and only one sign has been given from the time of Jesus' resurrection until his return—the death and resurrection of Jesus. — Douglas Sean O'Donnell, *Matthew: All Authority in Heaven and on Earth, ed. R. Kent Hughes, Preaching the Word* (Wheaton, IL: Crossway, 2013), 339.

19. What do you want to recall from today's conversation?

20. How can we support one another in prayer this week?

Lesson #13, Matthew 13.1 - 13
Good Questions Have Groups Talking
www.joshhunt.com

Matthew 13.1 - 13

OPEN

Let's each share your name and… have you done any farming or gardening?

DIG

1. Let's make sure we all have the story straight. Someone summarize this story for us.

Before we look at the three ways of disaster represented by these three sorry soils, I want us to grasp that there are two different perspectives to take in interpreting Jesus' interpretation, both of which are necessary. One perspective is to view the three ways of disaster from an internal perspective, from the soils' point of view, so to speak. That is, identifying the problem in the soil's hardness, shallowness, and self-indulgence, what James Montgomery Boice called the hard heart, the shallow heart, and the strangled heart.5 Another perspective is to view the three ways of disaster from an external perspective, identifying the problem from the outside—in terms of Satan (the birds of v. 4), persecutions, trials, and temptations. — Douglas Sean O'Donnell, *Matthew: All Authority in Heaven and on Earth, ed. R. Kent Hughes, Preaching the Word* (Wheaton, IL: Crossway, 2013), 365.

Parable of the Sower

Jesus often spoke in parables while teaching. He used this parable to differentiate between types of people who hear God's Word.

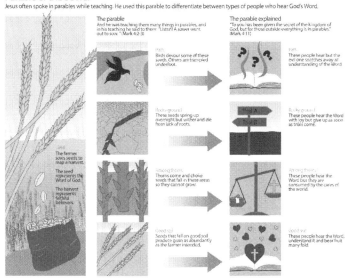

The parable
And he was teaching them many things in parables, and in his teaching he said to them "Listen! A sower went out to sow." (Mark 4:2-3)

The parable explained
"To you has been given the secret of the kingdom of God, but for those outside everything is in parables." (Mark 4:11)

Path
Birds devour some of these seeds. Others are trampled underfoot.

Path
These people hear but the evil one snatches away all understanding of the Word

Rocky ground
These seeds spring up overnight but wither and die from lack of roots.

Rocky ground
These people hear the Word with joy but give up as soon as trials come.

Among thorns
Thorns come and choke seeds that fall in these areas so they cannot grow.

Among thorns
These people hear the Word but they are consumed by the cares of the world.

Good soil
Seeds that fall on good soil produce grain as abundantly as the farmer intended.

Good soil
These people hear the Word, understand it and bear fruit many fold.

The farmer sows seeds to reap a harvest.

The seed represents the Word of God.

The harvest represents faithful believers.

2. We always want to read the Bible for application. Imagine you are reading this section in your Quiet Time. What would you say the application is?

This parable has two applications. Primarily, it speaks of how we hear the Word. Secondarily, it gives understanding about how we share the Word. In verse 9, Jesus says, "Whoever has ears to hear, let him hear." Tune in! Think through. Listen up!

A former television news producer conducted a most intriguing survey. Following one broadcast, he sent a crew to survey people who watched the show in its entirety, which at that time consisted of nineteen stories in the thirty-minute broadcast. Fifty-one percent of those who watched the entire half-hour broadcast could not remember a single story. His conclusion was that people don't listen, and a decision was made at that time to simplify news programming.

So, too, understanding the limited attention span of humanity, Jesus taught in simple, unforgettable, powerful parables—one of His most well known being the Parable of the Sower. — Jon Courson, *Jon Courson's Application Commentary* (Nashville, TN: Thomas Nelson, 2003), 93.

3. Verse 3. "Parable" is a familiar word to those of us in church world. What exactly does it mean?

The use of parables was the way people communicated when they wanted to arouse curiosity and excite interest. They wouldn't use guitars or humor, but rather they would use parables—little stories with big messages. The word "parable" comes from parabole in Greek. The Greek word para means "alongside," while ballo means "to cast, or to throw." Thus, the word "parable" means "casting alongside." Parabolic teaching places a story alongside a truth or a principle. As you study parables, realize this: The lost and the lazy will not understand them, but for those who are interested in truth, they are wonderfully illuminating. — Jon Courson, *Jon Courson's Application Commentary* (Nashville, TN: Thomas Nelson, 2003), 92.

4. Just for fun... let's see how many parables of Jesus we can recall.

Christ's words were always picturesque. He spoke of sheep among wolves (Matt. 10:16), of camels creeping through the eye of a needle (Matt. 19:24), of people trying to remove specks from other people's eyes while planks were in their own (Matt. 7:5). He referred to a house divided against itself, destined to fall down (Mark 3:25), of throwing children's bread to dogs (Mark 7:27). He warned against the "yeast" of the Pharisees (Mark 8:15). Strictly speaking, however, these imaginative pictures are not stories. The stories Jesus told all fall into a particular category of story known as parables.

A parable is a story from real life or a real-life situation from which a moral or spiritual truth is drawn. Examples are abundant: the prodigal son (Luke 15:11–32), the good Samaritan (Luke 10:25–37), the Pharisee and the tax collector (Luke 18:9–14), the wedding banquet (Matt. 22:1–14; Luke 14:15–24), the sheep and the goats (Matt. 25:31–46), and others, including the parables of the kingdom that we have come to now (Matt. 13:1–52). By my count there are twenty-seven parables in the four Gospels, though some are similar and may merely be different versions of the same root story. — James Montgomery Boice, *The Gospel of Matthew* (Grand Rapids, MI: Baker Books, 2001), 228–230.

5. What is the difference between a parable and a fable?

Parables differ from fables in that a fable is not a real situation. An example of a fable is any of Aesop's stories, in which animals talk. In those stories the animals are simply people in disguise. Parables also differ from allegories, since in an allegory each or nearly each detail has a meaning. The best-known and probably the most successful allegory ever written is John Bunyan's Pilgrim's Progress. But there are others. C. S. Lewis's Chronicles of Narnia are essentially allegories. In the parables of Jesus not every detail has a meaning. In fact, to try to force meaning into each of the details produces strange and sometimes even demonstrably false doctrines. Parables are merely real-life stories from which one or possibly a few basic truths can be drawn. — James Montgomery Boice, *The Gospel of Matthew* (Grand Rapids, MI: Baker Books, 2001), 230.

6. Verse 10ff. Why did Jesus teach in parables?

As verses 10–15 make clear, Jesus adopted the use of parables at this specific stage in his ministry for the deliberate purpose of withholding further truth about himself and the kingdom of heaven from the crowds.

Why should he do that? The answer is that masses of people had rejected him (Matt. 11:16–24) and therefore could not understand the deeper things that he now needed to reveal about the kingdom. The disciples, on the other hand, had begun to believe on him and were looking to him for teaching. Therefore, he taught his lessons in parables and then explained the stories to them. In fact, as Matthew makes clear, from this point on the explanation of the parables is always given to the disciples alone and never to the crowds. — James Montgomery Boice, *The Gospel of Matthew* (Grand Rapids, MI: Baker Books, 2001), 230–231.

7. Who is the farmer in this story?

When I sat down to study this passage, I first made a simple chart with two columns. In the left column I listed the main details in the parable as given in verses 3–9. I listed the sower, the seeds, and the four soils. Then, in the right column, looking at verses 18–23, I listed how Jesus interpreted these various details.

In doing this I first discovered that the "sower" mentioned in verse 3 is not identified. Having noticed this omission, and believing there was some purpose for it, I concluded the "sower" must symbolize one or all of the following. It could be that the "sower" refers to God, for at times this language is used of him in the Old Testament. Or it could be that the "sower" refers to Jesus, for when Jesus explains the Parable of the Weeds he says in 13:37, "The one who sows the good seed is the Son of Man." Or it could be that the "sower" represents any preacher, parent, or Sunday school teacher— that is, anyone and everyone who sows the word. Our Lord's lack of interpretation regarding the "sower," which I think is intentional, allows for an expanded application. The "sower" could include or does include God, his Son, and any and all gospel workers. — Douglas Sean O'Donnell, *Matthew: All Authority in Heaven and on Earth, ed. R. Kent Hughes, Preaching the Word* (Wheaton, IL: Crossway, 2013), 364.

8. What is the seed?

As I worked my way down this chart, I noticed next that the "seeds" (cf. Isaiah 55:10, 11) mentioned in this parable symbolized "the word" (six times) and more specifically "the word of the kingdom" (v. 19). This is just Jesus' way of saying "the gospel"—the good news to the nations of the establishment of Jesus' sovereign rule by means of his death and resurrection. The "seed" is the gospel. — Douglas Sean O'Donnell, *Matthew: All Authority in Heaven and on Earth, ed. R. Kent Hughes, Preaching the Word* (Wheaton, IL: Crossway, 2013), 364.

9. What is the gospel? How would you summarize it?

First, what it is not: it is not the minimum requirements for how to go to Heaven when you die. It not the idea that if you pray this little prayer your sins are forgiven and you can be assured a place in Heaven.

It is the gospel of the kingdom. It is the gospel of, "Your will be done on earth as it is in Heaven." It is the good news that this world can become like Heaven. It is the good news that you can live a Spirit-filled life that is marked by love, joy, peace, patience... Your life this week can be a little more like Heaven. God wants to use you to make this world more like Heaven. It will never be completely like Heaven, but it can move radically in that direction. The earth like Heaven. Now that is good news. That is the gospel.

10. What is the first soil like?

The first type of soil represents the hard heart, of which there are many today as well as in Christ's time. It is described as soil along the path (v. 4). This ground has been trampled down by the many feet that have passed that way over scores of years. Because the soil is hard, the seed that falls there merely lies on the path and does not sink in, and the birds (which Christ compares to the devil or the devil's workers) soon snatch it away. What is it that makes the human heart hard? There can be only one answer: sin. Sin hardens the heart, and the heart that is hardened sins even more broadly and deliberately.

This type of person is described in the first chapter of Romans. The person begins by suppressing the truth about God that may be known from nature (vv. 18–20), plunges into the spiritual ignorance and degradation that inevitably follows (vv. 21–31), and at last comes not only to practice the sins of evil persons but to approve of them as well (v. 32). Here we see both halves of the circle: Sin leads to a rejection of God and God's truth, and the rejection of truth leads to even greater sin. What is it that leads such a person to reject the truth of God in the first place? According to Paul, it is a determined opposition to the nature of God himself, which the apostle describes as human "godlessness and wickedness" (Rom. 1:18). — James Montgomery Boice, *The Gospel of Matthew* (Grand Rapids, MI: Baker Books, 2001), 232.

11. Why do some shut their minds to hearing of the gospel?

There are the hearers with shut minds. There are people into whose minds the word has no more chance of gaining entry than the seed has of settling into the ground that has been beaten hard by many feet. There are many things which can shut people's minds. Prejudice can make them blind to everything they do not wish to see. The unteachable spirit can erect a barrier which cannot easily be broken down. The unteachable spirit can result from one of two things. It can be the result of pride which does not know that it needs to know; and it can be the result of the fear of new truth and the refusal to adventure on the ways of thought. Sometimes an immoral character and a particular way of life can shut the mind. There may be truth which condemns the things that an individual loves and which accuses the things that he or she does; and many refuse to listen to or to recognize the truth which condemns them, for there are none so blind as those who deliberately will not see. — William Barclay, *The Gospel of Matthew, Third Ed., The New Daily Study Bible* (Edinburgh: Saint Andrew Press, 2001), 70.

12. What is the second soil like?

The stony ground was not ground filled with stones; it was what was common in Palestine, a thin skin of earth on top of an underlying shelf of limestone rock. The earth might be only a very few inches deep before the rock was reached. On such ground, the seed would certainly germinate; and it would germinate quickly, because the ground grew speedily warm with the heat of the sun. But there was no depth of earth; and, when it sent down its roots in search of nourishment and moisture, it would meet only the rock, and would be starved to death and quite unable to withstand the heat of the sun. — William Barclay, *The Gospel of Matthew,*

Third Ed., *The New Daily Study Bible* (Edinburgh: Saint Andrew Press, 2001), 68.

13. Look down at verse 20 where Jesus is explaining this parable. What did Jesus mean by the phrase, "receives it with joy"?

Years ago I remember hearing a story about Martyn Lloyd-Jones, one of the great preachers of the last century. One day after Lloyd-Jones preached a powerful sermon, an unbeliever came up to him and said, "Dr. Lloyd-Jones, I must tell you that if you would have given an altar call at the end of your message I certainly would have come forward. I would have believed." Lloyd-Jones replied, "If you don't want Jesus five minutes after the service is over, then I assure you that you didn't truly want him at any point during my sermon." Now perhaps that is stronger than you would put it. But the point is a good one.

The true test of discipleship is not whether or not one received the gospel with joy at some datable moment in history. The true test of discipleship is whether or not one picks up his cross and follows Jesus, not for one day or two weeks or three months or four years, but until Jesus calls him home. The true Christian is not like a cut flower that a husband gives to his wife, a flower quite beautiful and alive for a week, but quite repulsive and dead after the unrelenting sun has beaten down upon it for a month. — Douglas Sean O'Donnell, *Matthew: All Authority in Heaven and on Earth, ed. R. Kent Hughes, Preaching the Word* (Wheaton, IL: Crossway, 2013), 367.

14. Note the phrase, "fall away" in verse 21. What is that talking about?

Have you ever known someone who has fallen away from the faith? I would imagine most of us have. And why in America, where there is so little persecution, is this true? Right now as you read this chapter, Christians in Sudan, China, and Iran are meeting secretly in homes, hotel rooms, and backrooms of businesses, and other Christians throughout the world are being beaten, tortured, and killed because they will not renounce Jesus Christ. As Blomberg notes, "In the twentieth century there were more martyrs for the Christian faith worldwide than in all nineteen previous centuries of church history combined." So why in America, where there is so little persecution, do so many people fall away from the faith? — Douglas Sean O'Donnell, *Matthew: All Authority in Heaven and on Earth, ed. R. Kent Hughes, Preaching the Word* (Wheaton, IL: Crossway, 2013), 367.

15. Why are there so many that fall away? How can we be sure it doesn't happen to us?

Part of the reason comes with the next bad surface—the love of this world (and especially the love of money). However, another part of the blame must be laid on those sloppy, sappy sowers—Christian evangelists who preach a half-seeded gospel, evangelists who never tell their disciples what Jesus repeatedly has been telling us in Matthew—that if you follow him, suffering will follow you. Today's evangelist says, "I need a thousand raised hands as a sign of success and God's blessing," but Jesus says, "Just give me twelve men who are willing to suffer and endure until the end, and I'll change the world." Perseverance through persecutions and triumphing through trials is what is necessary, through the power of God's might. Endurance is part of the basics of Christianity: "But the one who endures to the end will be saved" (10:22; 24:13).

So the first bad surface is "the path" (the person who cannot hold on to the gospel because he is inwardly hard and thus outwardly easy prey). The second bad surface is the "rocky ground" (the person who is so inwardly shallow that he outwardly cannot withstand the testing of his faith). The third bad surface is the thorn-infested soil. Concerning this soil Jesus says, "As for what was sown among thorns, this is the one who hears the word, but the cares of the world and the deceitfulness of riches choke the word, and it proves unfruitful" (v. 22).

The person described is inwardly self-indulgent and thus outwardly choked by worldly concerns. Put differently, this person cares too little about his soul because he cares too much about the world. For him the good seed never grows, but the thorns, which represent his worldly attachments, certainly do. Two thorns in particular grow, and they grow from the same root system. One thorn is "the cares of the world," and the other is "the deceitfulness of riches."

Both have at their root the love of money. Both have to do with not trusting God always and ultimately. You cannot serve both God and money. If you trust and treasure money above all, when you don't have enough of it your heart will be flooded with all sorts of anxieties. But if you trust and treasure money above all and you have a lot of it, then your problems are solved, right? Wrong! Then you have a bigger problem: you won't see your need for God and his grace, provision, and salvation. — Douglas Sean O'Donnell, Matthew: All Authority in Heaven and on Earth, ed. R. Kent Hughes, Preaching the Word (Wheaton, IL: Crossway, 2013), 367–368.

16. What kind of person does the third soil represent?

The thorny ground was deceptive. When the sower was sowing, the ground would look clean enough. It is easy to make a garden look clean by simply turning it over; but in the ground still lay the fibrous roots of the couch grass and the ground elder and all the perennial pests, ready to spring to life again. Every gardener knows that the weeds grow with a speed and a strength that few good seeds can equal. The result was that the good seed and the dormant weeds grew together; but the weeds were so strong that they throttled the life out of the seed. — William Barclay, *The Gospel of Matthew, Third Ed., The New Daily Study Bible* (Edinburgh: Saint Andrew Press, 2001), 68–69.

17. What keeps this third soil from being good soil? Be specific.

There are the hearers who have so many interests in life that often the most important things get crowded out. It is characteristic of modern life that it becomes increasingly crowded and increasingly fast. We become too busy to pray; we become so preoccupied with many things that we forget to study the word of God; we can become so involved in committees and good works and charitable services that we leave ourselves no time for him from whom all love and service come. Our work can take such a hold that we are too tired to think of anything else. It is not the things which are obviously bad which are dangerous. It is the things which are good, for the 'second best is always the worst enemy of the best'. It is not even that we deliberately banish prayer and the Bible and the Church from our lives; it can be that we often think of them and intend to make time for them, but somehow in our crowded lives never get round to it. We must be careful to see that Christ is not pushed into the sidelines of life. — William Barclay, *The Gospel of Matthew, Third Ed., The New Daily Study Bible* (Edinburgh: Saint Andrew Press, 2001), 71.

18. What made the good soil good?

If we could return to my chart and visualize the four soils in the left column and their interpretation in the right, what I found to be most remarkable was that for each soil or type of response Jesus essentially begins with the words "the one who hears the word" (vv. 20, 22, 23), or as it is in verse 19, "When anyone hears the word …" The difference between the soils is not hearing. They all hear. All four soils hear the word and to some extent or for some period of time accept it. Even the first soil is for a time on "the path" (v. 4)—i.e., the seed is "sown in his heart" (v. 19). The one difference between the three bad soils and the one good soil is that the latter "bears fruit" (v. 23; cf. v. 8).

There are vital differences between the first three bad surfaces and the last good soil, between the three bad hearers and the good hearer. The good hearer, who is neither hard nor shallow nor self-indulgent, welcomes the word immediately so it cannot be snatched away by Satan, welcomes it deeply so it is not withered by persecution, and welcomes it exclusively so other concerns do not strangle it. Then he bears fruit! He is not just a "hearer of the word" but a "doer" of the word (James 1:23). He bears fruit, a harvest of "love, joy, peace, patience, kindness, goodness, faithfulness, gentleness, self-control" (Galatians 5:22, 23), as well as a harvest of humility, prayerfulness, heavenly-mindedness. He lives a life of consistent obedience to the commands of Christ, a steadfast commitment to the will of God in Heaven on earth. — Douglas Sean O'Donnell, *Matthew: All Authority in Heaven and on Earth, ed. R. Kent Hughes, Preaching the Word* (Wheaton, IL: Crossway, 2013), 370.

19. Do the first three soils represent shallow, lukewarm, half-hearted Christians? Are they Christians at all?

Taken at face value, the message of the parable of the soils is clear: of four soils, only one is good. Only one produces fruit, and thus it alone is of any value to the farmer. This good soil pictures the believer. The weedy soil and the shallow soil are pretenders. The soil by the wayside is an absolute rejecter.

Fruit, not foliage, is the mark of true salvation. Those who miss that point confuse the meaning of the parable. Much has been written in recent years attempting to argue that the shallow soil or weedy soil represent true believers, albeit unproductive ones. For example, Zane Hodges writes:

> From the roadside—and from the roadside alone—the Word of God had been retrieved. By the Saviour's own explicit observation this retrieval was for the purpose that salvation might not occur. Here, but here alone, Satan had triumphed completely.... The inference from this was plain. Into all of the remaining hearts, whatever the character of their soil, new life had come.

That misses the point completely. The seed in the parable is not symbolic of eternal life; it is the message of the gospel. The sprouting of the seed in the shallow soil and the weedy soil simply means that the Word had been received and had begun to operate, not that eternal life had been conferred. Warren Wiersbe understands the issue clearly:

> It is important to note that none of these first three hearts [the soil by the wayside, the shallow soil, and the weedy soil] underwent salvation. The proof of salvation is not listening to the Word, or having a quick emotional response to the Word, or even cultivating the Word so

that it grows in a life. The proof of salvation is fruit, for as Christ said, "Ye shall know them by their fruits" (Matt. 7:16).

Indeed, fruit is the ultimate test of true salvation. In the harvest, weedy soil is no better than the hard road or shallow ground. All are worthless. Seed sown there is wasted, and the ground is fit for nothing except burning (cf. Heb. 6:8). It cannot picture salvation. — John F. MacArthur Jr., *The Gospel according to Jesus: What Does Jesus Mean When He Says "Follow Me," Electronic ed.* (Grand Rapids, MI: Academic and Professional Books, Zondervan Pub. House, 2000).

20. Having looked at this parable a little more deeply, what would you say are the applications for us?

A major lesson to be learned from the parable is that we should not be overly concerned about the indicated response or lack of it when we are proclaiming the gospel. We cannot force the response. The laborer is simply to share Christ in the power of the Holy Spirit, leaving the results with God. The sower sows the Word of God; the hearing and the responding are outside his responsibility.

Yet another truth that surfaces is that good soil will multiply fruit. Today's convert is tomorrow's disciple and next year's laborer and leader. The spiritual multiplication through the effort of laborers is God's perfect plan for reaching the world. — Bill Hull, *Jesus Christ, Disciplemaker, 20th Anniversary Edition* (Grand Rapids, MI: Baker Books, 2004), 166.

21. How can we pray for one another this week?

Made in the USA
Columbia, SC
26 March 2023